THE JOKE'S OVER, YOU CAN COME BACK NOW

THE JOKE'S OVER, YOU CAN COME BACK NOW

HOW THIS WIDOW PLOWED THROUGH GRIEF AND SURVIVED

LAURIE BURROWS GRAD

Photographs from the family collection of Laurie Burrows Grad. Additional photographs courtesy of Alex Berliner.

Cover and book design by The Lincoln Avenue Workshop

ISBN: 1981137866
ISBN-13: 978-1981137862
Library of Congress Control Number: 2017918336

Published by
LBG PRODUCTIONS, INC.
Los Angeles, California

TESTIMONIALS

At the Center for Complicated Grief we believe grief is the form love takes when someone we love dies. Laurie Grad's book brings this idea to life. Of course, it's not the only book to do that. Many people write their way through a strange new world, infused with absence and filled with pain, expected and surprising. But I don't think there is another such book filled with recipes—real ones—that are delicious, by the way. Her recipes, both literal and figurative, for widowhood are not just for widows. Friends and family members of bereaved spouses— in fact anyone wanting an exceptionally thoughtful and wry look at many of the daunting challenges of this universal experience will find Laurie's descriptions honest, lucid and engaging. You will want to meet her.
— M. KATHERINE SHEAR. M.D, DIRECTOR,
CENTER FOR COMPLICATED GRIEF,
COLUMBIA SCHOOL OF SOCIAL WORK

What do we do with loss? What do we do with profound loss? With courage, honesty, and HUMOR, my friend Laurie asks those tough questions and helps us find some answers.
—JOEY McINTYRE

Everyone who knew Laurie and Peter Grad admired their marriage. It was the gold standard. Laurie's honest coming to terms with her grief after Peter's sudden death makes for compelling and (I'm not kidding) funny reading. Helpful for both men and women to learn how to speak the language of loss.
—LISA BIRNBACH

I dedicate this book to my sweet Peter.
You may have been stolen from me by death,
but I will never, ever stop loving you.
You are my best friend, my cherished love,
and my soul mate for all eternity.

ACKNOWLEDGMENTS

This book could not have been written without the help of my posse of friends. I would like to particularly thank:

My literary gurus Lisa Birnbach and Jane Heller, for their judicious and wise edits of my first blogs. They have continually guided me on the right path, for which I will be forever grateful.

Diane Worthington for filling Peter's void by calling me and letting me know I was not alone. She and her sweet husband, Mikey were instrumental in my journey.

My "bestest" pal, Betsy Castenir, for patiently listening to me cry and whine and then teaching me to find laughter again.

My dear friend, Kathleen Gray, for moving into the void and helping me through the tough times. We forged ahead together by talking nonstop on our daily walks, sharing dinners served on trays, and watching Netflix like two very comfy old Jews.

My sweet friends, Karen and Gary Richman, for easily turning our date nights of four into the three amigos.

To Suzi Dietz, for her amazing ability to always look on the bright side of life, and for teaching me how to fight against those unscrupulous, immoral bad guys in this crazy world.

To Barbara Tenenbaum, aka BT, for helping me realize I needed to get out of my large house and easing my way towards apartment living. Her task was helped when the alarm went off in the middle of the night and my only ammunition was a can of Easy Off!

To Hearst Magazine Publishing leader Ellen Levine, for her wise counsel and unwavering support throughout my writing career.

Nick Santise for his gentle guidance in designing this book inside and out.

My wise therapist, Fredda Wasserman, for gently facilitating my journey, while understanding that I had to use humor to get me through the pain.

My dear son Nick Grad and his wife Carolyn Bernstein, for their support, and to my astoundingly wonderful grandkids Lucas and Georgia for keeping me laughing.

To my brother Jimmy Burrows for delivering the best line at the Memorial "what do you say to someone who sleeps with your sister." And, to Peter's sister Susan Baerwald for keeping me sane with weekly sushi lunches.

And to all the other pals including Andrea and Bill, Beth, Betsy II and Bruce, Bud, Carrie, Catherine and Allan, Cinder and Scott, Dawn, Elizabeth, Elsie, Fredi, Gina, Heidi, Julie, Leslie, Lorraine, Mara, Midori, Mira, Pamela, Peggy, Ro, Sara, Skip and Toni, Susan, Suzanne and Rob, Teri, and many more. You know who you are! You were there for me, and are still there for me on my long journey without Peter.

FOREWORD

"GRIEF IS A SLOW and steady marathon" is only one of the many beautifully expressed and accurate observations Laurie makes in this deeply felt, heart-wrenching, and at the same time very witty book. Laurie and Peter were rarely apart during their long marriage, so the shock of his unexpected heart attack, elicited from her an earthquake of outrage, fury, sadness, and of course GRIEF!

Her bravery, unbridled honesty, and lack of fear to forge ahead, while taking me, and others on her journey into the profundity of grief, astounds me. This book is a revelation! Laurie lets it rip like no other I've read. Hers is not the American way of burying grief deep inside. Laurie lets her grief fly with guts, hilarity, and wisdom! How grateful I am that she gave me the opportunity to claim my grief in a way I didn't think was possible, letting loose everything unexpressed. On her journey, she has unearthed every nook and cranny available to heal herself, and by extension, helped to heal me and others. This book is an eye-opener and an inspiration. I encourage every person who has lost a spouse, or loved one, to devour it! You'll laugh, cry, experience catharsis, and feel so much better!

—BLYTHE DANNER

INTRODUCTION

ON AUGUST 1, 2015, my husband, Peter, and I were on our annual vacation in Vail, Colorado, with the same group we had been meeting there for over twenty years. We always looked forward to these trips, seeing old friends from our college days, attending the ballet, and being in the fresh mountain air, even though breathing at altitude is a constant challenge in Vail. On that Friday, Peter played eighteen holes of golf and was exhilarated. He hadn't been well for a while, and he was thrilled that he could play golf with his buddies and watch the ball fly for miles in the altitude. I hiked with my girlfriends, and then our group went to the amphitheater for a magical outdoor concert. After the concert, Peter wasn't feeling great, but we chalked it up to the altitude. When in Vail, blame it on the altitude! We managed to go to dinner, where he picked at his food (not a common thing for Peter, whose favorite occupation was eating). We then returned to the house and both fell asleep quickly. In the middle of the night, I was awakened to hear Peter screaming: "I can't breathe. I can't breathe." He was writhing around in the bed, so I ran upstairs and told my friends to call 911. I told him over and over to stay with me. With tears streaming down my face and my heart racing, I asked him my name, and he said "Laurie." I asked him my name again, and he said something unintelligible. My heart stopped then because I knew his mind was gone. Then he slipped away right in front of me. By the time the paramedics came, I knew Peter had vanished.

One minute he was laughing and happy, and the next minute, my beloved husband of forty-seven years was dead. I was in shock. I fell to the floor with heaving sobs, not able to comprehend what had happened.

Peter's health was continually precarious, but he always rallied. This time he didn't. Suddenly, out of nowhere, my life, as I knew it, was over. The Old English root of the word bereavement means "to rob." I was robbed of my husband, my life, my existence.

When I married Peter at the age of twenty-three, I knew I had found the person who would cherish me unconditionally, in sickness and in health. We met on October 17, 1967. I was wearing a rabbit miniskirt and go-go boots. He was wearing khakis and penny loafers. It was love at first sight. We were engaged two months later, and married two months after that. I knew I had found the man who wouldn't stop pinching my ass (even though I am deficient in that region), who wouldn't stop reaching for my boobs (I am much better in that area), and who wouldn't stop saying that he had lived life fully with the woman he loved and had no regrets—and that was before Zoloft!

We had the most amazing marriage. I don't know many marriages where couples spend so much time together and still want more. We were best friends, and we worshipped each other. Every time I saw his face come through the door, I sighed like a lovestruck schoolgirl. I went through some serious illnesses with Peter, but he always recovered. He bounced back and became stronger. But this time, he didn't bounce back. He didn't come back to me, and I was beyond desolate. Widowhood is dreadful, and I didn't want to be a member of this detestable club. Jane Austen's nineteenth-century widows are clothed in black with bustles and veils. That was not me! It couldn't be me? I just couldn't be a widow? Oh, how I would prefer to be a golf widow.

But the reality is that I was unexpectedly thrust into widowhood, where I lost my husband and my social status all in one event! I have discovered that women today are more open about the pain of childbirth than they are about the pain of grief. We used to hide the reality of childbirth, but now we talk openly about ways to help each other cope with the pain. Years ago, we talked in hushed tones about cancer as the c-word, never wanting to say it aloud and give it credence. Plastic surgery was another unmentionable subject, but today we talk openly about our fillers and scars. Even antidepressants were taboo subjects, but today, people proudly talk about their doses of Prozac and Lexapro!

A month after Peter died, I put all my feelings into a treatise called "Demoted to Lunch: The Underbelly of Grief." *The Huffington Post* ran it, and it went viral. It seems no one talks with raw emotion and humor about grief.

Facebook COO Sheryl Sandberg changed the landscape for widows in her beautiful treatise, written thirty days after her beloved husband died. She said, "When I am asked 'How are you?' I stop myself from shouting, 'My husband died a month ago, how do you think I am?' When I hear 'How are you today?' I realize the person knows that the best I can do right now is to get through each day." I met Sheryl a few months after Peter died. She was open and encouraging. She kindly assured me that acute grief would not last. She told me to keep blogging online, which would help me in my process. I am so grateful to Sheryl for opening the door for me to talk honestly about grief.

The response to my blog gave me the courage to journalize my feelings into a diary chronicling my broken heart. In my mind, I called this my "journey through grief." Writing was the one outlet that kept me sane. When I was upset or stressed, I wrote, and it helped me to come to grips with my feelings. I now have a regular blog on *The Huffington Post*, and it gets the most amazing comments: "This is everything I wish I could tell people. I lost my husband of fifteen years almost two months ago. He was only thirty-seven. This article touches on everything I wish people could know." Or: "It is hard to talk about grief. At times, you don't want to overburden anyone and really how could they understand unless they have been there?" And: "It is just amazing how you can write what I am feeling. You have to compile these into a book!"

I have devoured book after book on the subjects of widowhood, grief, and loss. Not one of the books on the market today connects with my experience. I can't abide by the hokey shibboleths and corny advice. No one talks about the status of a successful woman who has lost her social standing. Not one of these books deals with the logistics of sudden death. Nobody addresses any of these problems with humor, pathos, and raw honesty. Not one talks about how your mascara runs or how your nose resembles Rudolph the Red-Nosed Reindeer.

This book will help you cope with sleeping, cooking for one, juggling finances, and handling all the practical aspects of widowhood. It is an honest and forthright documentation of what occurred when I suddenly became a widow. It is the definitive self-help guide for widows of any age dealing with the loss of a loved one. It will also be a fantastic resource for those who are supporting a widow and need to know the right things to say and ways to help them most effectively.

Seventy is the new fifty today! The aging baby boomers are now seniors coping with the loss of their beloved spouses. We baby boomers are a different generation from our parents. We exercise, eat better, take care of our bodies, and generally live fuller lives into our seventies and eighties. Sadly, we know that women are most likely to outlive their husbands. Even those who are financially and technically savvy need a companion, a buddy who's been through it all and can guide them step by step through their journey of grief. Women need to know how to keep themselves healthy during the tough times and how to say a resounding no, when necessary. This book will take those suffering a loss through all the stages and counsel them on the best way to put one foot in front of the other on this arduous journey—Grief 101!

I am a food writer by profession. Recipes are my thing, and when I get stressed, I need to cook. It took several months for me to find my joy of cooking again. Slowly I ventured into the kitchen to make dinners for friends who took me out. Recipe by recipe I clawed my way back into my kitchen and found peace there. Because good food is so much a part of my life, I want to pepper my book with recipes that give me comfort and strength. I hope you will enjoy the treats I have included in this book.

The Joke's Over; You Can Come Back Now: How This Widow Plowed Through Grief and Survived is an informative and inspirational go-to book for a person thrust into widowhood. Widows do not lack bravery or the motivation to move forward. They just need to be equipped with the appropriate knowledge to help them on their journey through grief. This book will help them navigate the turbulent waters of grief. There has never been a book for those in grief, combining information, humor, recipes, and specific helpful tasks. Giving back has been part of my recovery after loss. Writing this book has helped me immensely, and knowing that I am helping others on their journeys through grief gives me a new purpose and helps me find my new normal, which I call "acceptably different."

—LAURIE BURROWS GRAD
WWW.LAURIEGRAD.COM

*If you would like to be the first to receive
my latest articles visit:*
LAURIEGRAD.COM/NEWSLETTER-SIGNUP

CONTENTS

YEAR ONE

Recipes included in the book

YEAR ONE

~~~~~~

SHOCK AND ALL
Demoted to Lunch

IN THE FIRST WEEK, the initial distress of your loss is so unbearable, that your body goes into shock mode. I believe that numbness sets in after you lose your spouse, because you can't fully conceptualize that your life has changed forever. If you didn't have the detachment from your new reality, the scariness of the experience would catapult you into a seizure of fear and anxiety so monumental, that you could not cope with the situation. This is the key reason that family and friends rally around you and keep you busy so you don't go down the road to "panic land."

Keeping busy is important in the initial stages. And busy you will be, just getting the funeral arrangements finalized, finding the documents you need, and beginning to take care of finances. In the first few weeks, my dear friends circled me like a posse. My amazing son and his family were there for me. My brother, Peter's sister, and all my friends rallied and brought more food than a human could consume. When you are in the initial stages of grief, you will have no appetite, but the food is there for others who want to help. My friends cared for me, hugged me on a regular basis, and held me in their arms as we cried together. All of this was a great comfort, but where was Petey to hear the stories? How could I go on without my partner?

I finally saw a grief counselor, two weeks after Peter died. She was comforting and nice and had an ample supply of tissues. I told her I have been demoted to lunch, as in "Oh, let's have lunch, Laurie, and talk about Peter," instead of "Oh, let's have dinner, Laurie, and talk

3

about politics," which is what people used to say when we were a couple. She doesn't laugh at my jokes but realizes that I need humor to get me through this. Who knew no one talks openly about the pain of grief? She asked me to describe it. I say it is like a weight tied around me and I feel submerged in water, unable to get to the surface. Is that a description or a pattern of torture?

I get daily calls from well-meaning folks asking how I am. My grief has given me a quick tutorial in what to say to mourners. I want them to ask me how I am doing this minute! There should be a pain barometer for grief. Doctors inquire about back pain all the time. Is it a five or a seven today? I was amazed when a friend said to me, "I know exactly what you are going through. My mother died six months ago." What people don't realize is that the loss of a spouse is different. When you lose a parent, you have siblings or family members to comfort you. When you lose a spouse, you lose your life partner and are mind-bogglingly alone.

The hardest thing about grief is to witness life moving on. People all around me continue to do their daily routines. The stock market keeps functioning; meteorologists predict the weather; time marches on. I cannot understand how I have lost Peter and the clocks have not stopped.

For my own sanity, I started to journalize on Day Eight. "Day Eight and it is worse. I start on Day Eight because I can't start on Day One. No one who has lost a spouse can start on Day One. I don't know how to move, or react, or sigh, or even breathe. I have lost my spirit, and the pain is unimaginable. It hurts like a knife in my heart. It cuts through my soul, and I don't want to be here without my love. I wake each day like the movie *Groundhog Day*, reliving the pain of my loss. I go to bed on drugs to ease my anxiety only to be jolted awake in the early morning hours to my new painful existence."

The strength of my grief was so pervasive that I felt it constantly without respite. When my son called, I was having one of my heaving-sob moments and admitted the depths of loneliness and sorrow to him. I carry this burden around without choice. Oh, how I wish I had gone first to avoid feeling the excruciating angst. But then my sweet love would have had to endure this pain, and it would have killed his heart.

I wish I weren't just "Jew-ish" and believed in an afterlife. I envy those whose religion comforts them through the pain.

I got a thoughtful note from a mother at my grandchild's school telling me some lovely things she saw in my marriage. Then she changed gears in midsentence and suggested I see a medium to ease my pain. I told her I would "see an extra small before a medium."

No one should look at grief before they must face it. But we should be prepared for its effect on our life. Maybe if we talk about grief more, it will lessen the pain when it happens?

IMPORTANT FINANCIAL FACTS FOR A WIDOW

RIGHT AFTER PETER DIED, I had assistance from my estate planners and advice from other widows, which helped immeasurably in coping with the necessary financial planning.

FIRST PRIORITY

- ➡ Locate the will.

- ➡ If you have an estate planner, they should be the first call you make.

- ➡ Let your accountants know immediately.

- ➡ Have the mortuary issue six to eight death certificates which you will need. Now that scanning is available, you might need fewer.

- ➡ Locate your spouse's birth certificate and his social security number.

- ➡ Find your marriage certificate.

- ➡ If any trusts have been set up, retrieve those papers.

- ➡ Notify your spouse's employer.

- ➡ Ascertain the location of a safe-deposit box and key.

- ➡ Contact your bank immediately.

➡ Ready a copy of your tax returns.

➡ Locate a list of passwords that your spouse used.

➡ Find your spouse's credit cards, and if they are not joint, notify the company. If you have a joint account, you do not need to notify them right away.

HOUSE AND VEHICLE INFORMATION

➡ If you own a home, find the real estate title and deeds.

➡ Find your spouse's car registration.

➡ If your spouse leased a car, find the lease and make plans to sell the car at CarMax, which will give you the best deal to pay off the lease.

➡ If you own a home or apartment, have a real estate person appraise your house or apartment.

➡ If you have a mortgage, let the company know that you want to change the account to your name.

➡ Call the utility companies. Both electric and gas will have to put the accounts in your name. You will need a death certificate to show them. This is very important!

INVESTMENTS

➡ Find all the stock statement information.

➡ Track down information on pension and retirement plans and IRAs.

➡ Uncover any credit-union information.

➡ Find any investment account statements and let them know of the death.

INSURANCE

➡ Discover if a life-insurance policy exists.

➡ Call your homeowner's and car insurance company to let them know of the death.

➡ Alert the long-term life-insurance company and discontinue that policy.

➡ Call Social Security. They are very helpful and will make it easy for you. If your spouse was on Medicare, they will help you with this as well.

➡ Notify any health-insurance companies of the death.

OTHER DETAILS

➡ Let any clubs or organizations know of the death. You can often sell back a membership in a club.

➡ Cancel your spouse's driver's license, which will remove the name from the department of motor vehicles, and which will help prevent identity theft.

➡ Immediately pay bills that need paying. Prioritize the others so that you can tackle them when you are better equipped for the task.

➡ Have a friend set up bill paying on your computer. If you can afford it, hire a reputable bookkeeper to teach you the ropes so that you can feel comfortable with this chore.

➡ Call the airlines to transfer any mileage from your spouse's account into yours.

➡ Order some note cards to thank people for their kindnesses.

➡ Organize a file of estate papers and numbers. Keep every receipt, including funeral expenses, catering, and fees to accountants, in one file.

➡ Begin to get a snapshot of your expenses so you can figure out your own finances.

The most important thing to remember is do not make any rash or quick decisions. Put everything on pause until you have enough time to focus and make rational decisions!

LETTER TO MY LOVE
Dear Peter...

A MONTH AFTER PETER died, my therapist suggested I write a letter to him. Talk about a hard exercise! This was both gut wrenching and oddly cathartic at the same time. I realized I was deep into the process of grief, and it helped me to trust in the movement of the process to help me put one foot in front of the other.

Dear Peter:

My first blog went up on The Huffington Post *this morning. The outpouring of emotion is heartening and heartbreaking at the same time. The sadness hits again with a vengeance, and I see you staring at me with those wonderful understanding eyes, so proud of everything I do. But where are you for the edits? Where are your deep, soft hugs of comfort? I miss you so much, each second of each day, and this letter just brings up all the pain.*

My grief therapist says I should write to you. So, I am writing a letter to you like a kid writes to Santa. The letter will never reach its recipient, but the writing is therapeutic. Maybe you will send me a message from the North Pole or wherever you are that you are OK?

Wherever I go, I see friends and acquaintances. Instead of hugs from them, I get sad, pouty faces, and it makes me nuts. I understand where they are coming from and appreciate that they care. Before you died, I would have done the sad, pouty face thing too. But now, I would just hug someone. I crave the contact of a hug and realize how I miss being hugged.

I have a wonderful story to tell you about our fantastic grandson. He often talks about his "Duke," the best grandfather ever. I took this seafood lover out to dinner the other night, and you would have been so proud of him. He started with a dozen oysters, followed by a bowl of Eastern steamers, and then tackled a lobster roll. I could see he was slowing down on the lobster roll. He said, "I'm doing a WWDD, LaLa." I said, "What's a WWDD?" He said, "It's a 'What would Duke do?'" He then proceeded to down the rest of the lobster in one shot.

The other day both grandkids slept over. I was having a sad moment in the morning, lying in bed with our granddaughter, and she said, "Come on, LaLa, it's time to make some cinnamon rolls." The kids are the joy that keeps me going.

I look at the hundreds of comments on my blog, and I see how others feel who have had this kind of loss. I love one comment from a person who said, "Without your former companion, you no longer have a mirror to reflect back to you, who you are, and what you want in life." That is where I am. I have lost my compass to go on and need you so. I know that I am glad I put this out there in all its raw emotion to let others know that it is OK to talk about grief, but it still hurts so much.

I miss you, my love.

Your ever-loving, Laurie

This exercise is very painful but also liberating and helpful. It is so important to get your feelings out and on paper. Try to write a letter to your loved one, or if you can't, try writing a letter to grief and then one back from grief. At this stage of your journey, you will be filled with so many emotions and will not be too happy with your not-so-great-friend grief. Putting this all on paper is a great exercise. It is important to chronicle your experience so that you can visualize your growth and progress.

A FEW TIPS TO INSPIRE A LETTER TO YOUR LOVED ONE

➡ I miss you when…

➡ I feel angry that…

➡ I am afraid that…

➡ I forgive you…

➡ I'm sorry for…

➡ One special memory I have of you is…

➡ If you were here at this moment, I would tell you…

➡ Thank you for…

➡ I regret that…

GRIEF AND THE LOSS OF CONTROL
The Search for Meaning in Loss

AS A CHILD OF divorce, I spent the majority of my life trying to control my surroundings to feel a sense of safety and security. I became a planner at a very early age. Planning and organizing kept my demons at bay and helped me cope with my life. Peter was the perfect partner. If I wanted to plan, he happily went with the program. Life was good until Peter died.

When Peter died, I lost control of my life. No matter how I tried to put the pieces back together, nothing fit. I felt as if my grief had control over me. I felt powerless to loosen its grip on my life. I was spinning out of control. Mundane things like showering or sleeping became impossible tasks. I was constantly exhausted from crying and from my loss. It took a while until I could find something to control in a positive way. I had to accept that grief was unpredictable and uncontrollable. Basically, I had to let go of my controlling behavior and learn new positive coping strategies. Negative coping would have been to numb the pain with drugs and alcohol.

Positive coping made me envision the wonderful work of Viktor Frankl in *Man's Search for Meaning.* Viktor Frankl was a trained psychiatrist and neurologist who spent three years in four Nazi concentration camps, an experience that helped him develop *logotherapy.* "*Logotherapy*" is a term derived from the words "logos," a Greek word that translates as "meaning," and "therapy," which is defined as "treatment of a condition, illness, or neurosis." Frankl observed that those who were able to survive the experience, were more likely to find meaning in their suffering. After the camps were liberated, Frankl resumed his work and published *Man's Search for Meaning*, a book centered on the premise that life has meaning under all circumstances, even the most miserable ones. Frankl felt humans were driven to find a sense of meaning and purpose in life. What I like most about Frankl's teachings, in the face of the worst possible adversity imaginable, is his concept that we have the freedom to find meaning in what we do, and what we experience, or at least in the outlook we choose, when faced with a situation of unalterable suffering.

If I take Frankl's premise to heart, I can see that in the face of my sorrow, I have the freedom to write down my feelings, and more importantly I have the freedom to blog about my emotions with others across the world. I have blogged my heart out to ease my own personal anguish, as well as to give voice to others experiencing deep grief. I am finding meaning in loss. I am finding positivity in sorrow. I am finding a way to keep living with purpose.

I am also looking to other parts of my life for purpose. I find that forging a stronger bond with my son and daughter-in-law has been immensely welcome and gratifying. Being with my grandkids has always been a win-win situation, and now it is so, in spades. We exchange love, warmth, humor, and joy, a quality that has often eluded me since my husband Peter died last year. I have learned a new acceptance and tolerance of others, that I consider a trusted attribute to have in my arsenal of purpose. I have always been hypervigilant, meaning my bull#&*t detector is on high alert as a protective mechanism. After Peter died I learned to be more open. I developed a sense of compassion so that I could empathize with other widows and widowers, as well as those who wanted to help me on my journey.

Dealing with my own loss has been unbearable. Sometimes grief literally takes my breath away so that the only way I can breathe is by sobbing, while gulping in bursts of air. But Frankl's teachings tell me to imagine the worst. So, I envision a scenario in which I die before Peter, and my body shakes uncontrollably at the thought of his suffering. My "meaning" is that I spared my sweet Peter this agony. Yes, I am paying a price by surviving and grieving, but I have found a strange comfort in knowing he didn't suffer this anguish. I am finding meaning in life even when confronted with a heartbreaking situation that is unalterable. I am trying to transform a tragedy into something meaningful. I am trying to make sense of my loss.

Frankl encourages us to recognize our grief and rage and to see our heartache as an experience in which it is possible to find some positivity from the pain. There is something in Frankl's "search for meaning" that is just evolving in my mind, and gives me the hope to go on. The nature of meaning is different for all of us. For me, writing is what keeps me going. This is my purpose that helps me to heal and to give a voice to others, letting them know that it is OK to grieve openly. If we must grieve, please let us do it openly, sobbing away our pain, without stigmas, taboos, and other hindrances.

> *Everything can be taken from a man but one thing:*
> *the last of the human freedoms—to choose one's attitude in any*
> *given set of circumstances, to choose one's own way.*
> —VIKTOR FRANKL

~~~~~~

WHO WILL ZIP UP MY DRESS NOW?
The Practical Aspects of Loss

BEING SUDDENLY WIDOWED BRINGS up a bunch of unforeseen practical things you can't do by yourself. In between bouts of tears, there are moments when I get dressed up and go out. My friends listened when I told them I needed to go out to dinner, not lunch, and I am now booked for a month with dinner and lunch plans. The other day I was slipping into a sheath dress, and there was no way I could get the zipper up. I live in a house and can't go half-dressed to the neighbors. I think I will invent a zipper pull for widows. Business op? It's number twelve on my to-do list. Being thrown into widowhood unexpectedly brings up a slew of new challenges. Hanging pictures solo is a complete pain. Putting on a tablecloth evenly is a feat. Moving a table or any type of furniture is agony. Lifting heavy groceries from the car is a trial. Bringing down my overstuffed heavy suitcase—the principessa still does not travel light—is a backbreaker.

Peter used to say that "some assembly required" were the worst words in the English language. If he had to put together a bookcase, it was a nightmare. He was not the hardware-store-loving type of guy. He would try, and then we would call our handyman for help to fix it again. But he did try, and occasionally he would fix something, and the grin on his face was priceless. All these practical tasks can be accomplished with the help of friends, but my biggest loss is not being able to share thoughts with Peter. After a dinner out, or after dinner in, or during any part of my day, I talked to Peter. While I was out in the daytime, we called each other five times a day with updates. That is the hole in my life. I can talk with friends and family, but it is not the wise counsel of my mind-blowingly kind husband. I miss that more than anything. Grief has changed my life forever. I am not the person I was a few months ago. What existed in my life before Peter died has been suddenly altered. Nothing is the same, nor will it ever be so. What was important to me before is meaningless now. I have new eyes to see, but the view is murky, with a treacherous road ahead. I will walk it, but it will take help and guidance.In the meantime, I am moving my tight sheath dresses to the back of my closet, and I have invested in a very high stepladder to replace all the light bulbs myself.

~~~~~~

THE WIDOW CONNECTION
Reaching Out to Other Widows

I HAVE BECOME CLOSER online with other widows. Old friends from my New York days, and several friends in Los Angeles, have been an unexpected comfort. They have known the pain, and by their example, I see a glimmer of hope. Being a widow is like living in a strange country where only a few people understand your special language of grief. It is a sign language of pain, and we are learning how to use it to get through the angst. My blogging online helps to give voice to this new language. I receive comments like "Thank you for sharing what is a new frontier." Another kindly remark was "I will assure you that the intensity of the pain will diminish, although you will always miss him. Take care of yourself, and grieve in your own time; don't let *anyone* tell you when you *should* be done!" Sheryl Sandberg posted her gratitude at Thanksgiving, a few months after her young husband suddenly died. She thanked friends and family for their support and expressed how their comfort helped her heal. "I also appreciate the many strangers who have reached out and shared their stories of tragedy, resilience, and rebirth."

After my first blog on *The Huffington Post*, another woman wrote, "Your blog 'Demoted to Lunch' is the perfect way to describe what I have been experiencing as a widow. This is beautifully written and relatable on so many levels. Thank you so much for this post, I feel comfort knowing I'm not the only one that feels this way." Another friend who lost her husband at a very young age wisely advised, "Somehow life gradually becomes bearable and even sweet again. But big events, an unexpected song, or a wedding or Bar Mitzvah will kill you every time…It's the ones you can't anticipate though that are devastating and the first holiday, anniversary without the one you love just have to be gotten through. You're doing it and then eventually you've gotten through the first of these things, and you learn how to protect yourself emotionally from some obligations that maybe you should occasionally just not fulfill." This is the widow connection. We need to heal by telling our stories and sharing our grief with others who are experiencing this journey.

Not all widows are as kind. One woman sends me e-mails that put me into a complete funk. She lost her husband several years ago and tells me it doesn't get better. I ask her if a group helped, and she tells me it does, but that her group is ending. I ask her about finding another group, and then I pull back and realize I am taking care of her. The one thing I need to do is take care of me! I can't be listening to people who pull me down. I have to grieve in my own way, on my own time. That is progress in itself.

My dear friend says I should take this negativity as a challenge. She is wise and right. She tells me I am naturally competitive and I should use this trait to prove others wrong. I like her positive outlook, and I like that I can be my own person. I will defy others and heal on my own terms, in my own way, and on my own timetable.

I have learned that the hardest part of a loved one dying is not that they are gone, but that you are still here. I am hoping I can one day find some healing in this journey of grief. I am clearly ready for a group. Wouldn't it be nice if all the men looked like James Garner and all the women looked like Camilla Parker Bowles? I could use that kind of support. A girl can dream, can't she? In truth, I think I would welcome the exchange of a group in a safe setting, allowing me a chance to be with others who are experiencing the same loss.

FINDING THE RIGHT GRIEF WHISPERER

A FEW WEEKS AFTER Peter died, I knew I needed help. I had never experienced grief of this intensity, and I was catapulted into unimaginable pain and sorrow. I was barely functioning and needed some heavy guidance. A lovely friend who had volunteered at a local bereavement center came to pay a condolence call. She had two names written out for me. I was so grateful. I knew I needed help pronto, so I called the therapist and made an appointment.

The grief therapist was calming and nurturing and took me on a journey using guided imagery, if that is indeed possible for me and my Type-A personality. The second grief counselor talked so low (hushed tones are de rigueur in the profession), I couldn't hear a word. I asked her to speak up over the flight pattern overhead. She moved her chair closer and continued to whisper. When she asked if I would continue for another session, I not so politely blurted out, "No!" I also went to a bonafide psychotherapist for a whole lot more money and cried for an hour. My friends tell me I can cry with them for nothing, and they will supply the wine.

I learned that grief counseling is an important tool and can make the difference in whether you spend a long time struggling with your loss or figure out tools and attitude changes that will sustain a healthier journey through grief. I went twice a week for several months; then when I started a support group, I cut back to once a week. Today, I go once a month as a refresher to keep me on a positive track. I am so lucky to have found a fabulous center and amazing woman who gets me. Finding the right grief therapist can be a difficult task. Here are some helpful guidelines.

TECHNIQUES FOR PICKING THE RIGHT BEREAVEMENT COUNSELOR

➡ The counselor should listen and support, but not pontificate about what you should do. "Shoulds" go out the window in grief!

➡ The counselor must look you in the eye and be engaged with you.

➡ The counselor should validate your feelings. The counselor should reinforce that what you are experiencing is natural and normal.

➡ The counselor should not ask, "How do you feel?" You feel like crap! If a counselor doesn't know this fundamental, they are not in the right biz!

➡ The counselor must resonate an attitude of caring and support.

➡ The counselor must help you figure out how you are going to get through the firsts. He or she can help you plan to diffuse the painful holidays and anniversaries that ominously stretch before you.

➡ The counselor shouldn't push too hard. Patience is indeed a virtue in grief therapy.

➡ The counselor might have you try guided imagery to help you get through your pain. Talking through relaxed states where your true feelings come to the surface can be effective.

➡ The counselor might suggest art therapy in your process. Doing a collage which illustrates your feelings can be a beneficial approach to dealing with grief.

➡ The counselor should speak loud enough so you can hear him or her. Whispering be damned!

YOU KNOW YOU HAVE PICKED
THE WRONG GRIEF THERAPIST WHEN

➡ The counselor tells you there are five stages of grief and you have to go through them in a regimented fashion. Each journey of grief is unique. We can't all fit into the same box!

➡ The counselor puts you into a cookie-cutter mold and says you have to follow the rules. Death makes all rules take a hike.

➡ The counselor tells you that grief has a time table. Grief is a natural process with no end date.

➡ The counselor tells you that you have to get over your grief. Really? You will always mourn the loss, and you will never get over it. You will adapt and learn to live with your loss, but you will never get over it.

➡ The counselor watches the clock, searches the room, yawns, and talks about themselves the whole time. OK, this is a big no for all therapists!

➡ The counselor tells you that you must keep busy to forget about your loss. Keeping busy is all right for a time. You need to take breaks and vacations from grief work, but you must face grief head on in order to effectively work through the process.

➡ The counselor tells you that you must let go of your loved one and say good-bye to the relationship. My relationship with Peter will last forever. I will *never* stop loving Peter.

➡ The counselor spouts clichés and platitudes, like "everything happens for a reason," or "you were lucky to have him at all." This is a dismissal of your emotions and feelings.

➡ The counselor tells you that "grief is the price we pay for love." This makes us feel like we are being punished for loving someone so deeply.

Nationwide Resources for Assistance with Grief: **Hospicefoundation.org** is a well-recognized organization for finding support.

From Columbia University's esteemed School of Social Work comes this site for help. **complicatedgrief.columbia.edu**

Healgrief.org has a mission to support those going through grief by offering a geographical location for those who need help. This organization uses technology to bring family, friends, and communities from around the globe to a local place to grieve and heal together.

Mastersincounseling.org/loss-grief-bereavement.html provides some of the best online resources for coping with grief and bereavement.

Griefnet.org is an excellent site for online grief support.

~~~~~~

TALKING TO THE BEREAVED 101
Please Don't Tell Me He's in a Better Place!

IT TRULY IRKS ME when people sermonize, "He's in a better place." I want to scream, "No, he's not! He should be sleeping beside me. That is a better place." I can think of a lot better places—like Cabo in the winter, Maine in the summer, or Italy any time. The best place would be alive and healthy and, of course, with me. If Peter were in a better place, he would be playing golf in Pebble Beach. That would truly be a better place. Then of course I would be a golf widow, instead of just a widow.

Which brings me to the subject of preaching clichés. I was a big-time offender before I learned the parameters of grief. I might have said the same banalities to console someone who had suffered a loss. But I have had a swift education, which I will now pass on to you.

Allow me to help you communicate with someone who has lost her or his life partner. Please do not tell us that "the living must go on!" Who can judge when any of us are ready to move on in our grief processes? Maybe others want me to move on so I will be my peppy self again and they can feel more at ease, but they will have to wait for as long as it takes.

"Everything happens for a reason," "It's all part of God's plan," and "God never gives you more than you can handle" are hard for me to fathom these days. Even if you think any of these bromides are true, I'm begging you not to tell us. Here's another doozy of a cliché: "All things must pass." You think? Peter passed away, and I am bereft. Who makes up this claptrap? Then there is, "He led a full life." Why are others the judges of what kind of life Peter had? How about "Be grate-ful you had him so long"? Right now, I miss him so much that nothing hurts more than this statement. "He would want you to get on with your life" is another. Sure, he would, but I'm pretty sure I know my husband better than anyone, and he would want me to grieve and heal first. "Time heals all wounds" is downright wrong. Time doesn't heal. Grieving heals. Crying heals—oh, and sometimes wine with crying too! One of the worst platitudes is "You'll find someone else." This belittles what we had; it belittles Peter, and it belittles me that I would be looking to replace my sweet love.

When Peter died, I suffered the greatest ordeal imaginable. I had a deep and intense loss, but I definitely didn't "lose" him. I, myself, am guilty of using the term "lose" on multiple occasions. I repeatedly said "I recently lost my husband" to friends, accountants, tax people, and even telemarketers. One day, when I was saying I had lost Peter, I real-ized it was not true. I didn't lose Peter. He died. I experienced a loss, but I didn't lose or misplace him. Saying that I lost him implies I am careless and makes me feel guilty that I wasn't vigilant enough to hold on to him. When you lose your keys, you expect to find them. When you lose your iPhone, you have the app Find My iPhone to locate your device. We expect to find the items we lose. Peter is not lost. He died, and there is no Find Peter app to download and locate my sweet love.

When there is a death, many people say that the person has "passed." This is another banality that is hard for me to stomach. I assume this came from the belief of passing from one life into a spiritual afterlife. It is clear to me that Peter passed the gravy; he passed a football when he was young; he passed a gallstone; he passed notes in class; and for sure he passed gas; but he didn't pass away. He died. He "slipped away" is another euphemism that I could easily avoid. I think of slipping away as escaping from being trapped. Peter didn't slip away willingly. His heart gave out, and he died.

I recognize that people want to comfort me. They may say things that are thoughtless, but they are trying to help. I have learned a toler-ance of others and am trying, through my blogging, to educate friends, family, and the public, on the best way to support me on my journey through grief.

I have good news and bad news. Below I have compiled the Top Ten Worst Things to Say to Someone in Grief (the bad news), followed by the good news, The Top Ten Best Things to Say.

THE TOP TEN WORST THINGS TO SAY TO SOMEONE IN GRIEF

1. He's in a better place. (A better place would be beside me now.)

2. Everything happens for a reason. (There is no rhyme or reason for this kind of loss.)

3. Time heals all wounds. (Time doesn't heal all wounds, although healing takes time.)

4. Try not to cry. He wouldn't want you to cry. (He'd be bawling his eyes out.)

5. It is time to put this behind you. (There is no timetable for grief.)

6. At least he lived a long life. If you think this is bad…(No comparisons, please.)

7. I know how you feel. (Do we ever really know how someone feels?)

8. Let me tell you about my own loss, which is similar to yours. (Please just listen and acknowledge my loss.)

9. Surely, you'll find someone. (This diminishes the person's loss and the loved one.)

10. You'll get through it. Be strong. (This tells people to hold on to their grief and not let it out.)

Now that we know what *not* to say to people who are grieving, here is a list of thoughtful remarks for those who want to know the kindest thing to say in times of grief.

THE TOP 10 SUGGESTIONS TO SAY
TO SOMEONE IN GRIEF

1. I am sorry for your loss. This is the tried and true easiest thing to say.

2. The best thing one can say is "I love you." Actually, a hug is the very best thing, since someone whose spouse dies, does not get hugs on a regular basis.

3. I wish I had the right words to comfort you. Just know that I care

4. I don't know how you feel, but I am available to help in any way I can.

5. I am always a phone call or e-mail away.

6. It's OK to cry, and it's OK to hurt.

7. My favorite memory of your loved one is…

8. Please let me know how I can help you.

9. How are you doing this minute?

10. Say nothing. (Just be with the person.)

At some of the darkest moments in my life, some people I thought of as friends deserted me—some because they cared about me and it hurt them to see me in pain; others because I reminded them of their own vulnerability, and that was more than they could handle. But real friends overcame their discomfort and came to sit with me. If they had not words to make me feel better, they sat in silence (much better than saying, "You'll get over it," or "It's not so bad; others have it worse") and I loved them for it.
—HAROLD KUSHNER, *LIVING A LIFE THAT MATTERS*

CONVERSATIONAL NARCISSISM

AFTER PETER DIED, I learned to sift through my friendships. I separated the wheat from the chaff in terms of my squad of devoted friends. I learned who would just sit, hug, and listen, and who would make comparisons and bring the focus completely back to themselves. This was my litmus test. For example, I might blubber, "This was the hardest thing I have ever gone through," and they would respond, "I know how you feel; I lost my beloved dog." Just from this simple exchange, I instantly knew this was not a friend I could count on for the long haul. Yes, I gave them the benefit of the doubt, and after several transgressions, I labeled them a "conversational narcissist" and someone with whom I could not share my feelings.

Sociologist Charles Derber coined the phrase "conversational narcissism" to describe the desire to monopolize a conversation and turn the focus on oneself. Derber went on to explain that there are two kinds of responses in conversations. The first is the shift response, and the second is the support response.

Examples:

Laurie: "I am missing Peter so much today."

SHIFT RESPONSE:

Conversational Narcissist: "I know how you feel because I feel worse than you."

SUPPORT RESPONSE:

Caring Person: "I bet you do. Please tell me more about your feelings."

Laurie: "My grief is endless. I just can't seem to get through it."

SHIFT RESPONSE:

Conversational Narcissist: "Be strong like me and pull yourself up by the bootstraps."

SUPPORT RESPONSE:

Caring Person: "I will be here for you as long as you need."

With a shift response, the conversational narcissist brings the conversation back to him- or herself. With a support response, the wise and compassionate person encourages the griever to share the story and just sits there and listens. As grievers, we need to tell our stories over and over, without judgment or interruptions. We need to keep telling the story to make it real. The more we tell the story, the more we understand our loss and the devastating reality of our situation. We need listeners, not critics. We need friends to hold our hands and just be there to get us through the toughest days. We need support and caring.

Once I discovered who were the conversational narcissists in my life, it became essential to remove them from my daily existence. I took care of my own needs by saying no to their invitations. Most of the time, without fuel for their own egos, they stopped calling, and I felt free of negative emotions. That in itself was a positive of Olympic proportions.

The other day I had a long conversation about Peter with a friend on the phone. The other person barely uttered a word, and at the end of the call, I thanked my dear and kind friend for helping me work things out. She hadn't really said a thing. All she did was listen and be supportive. Now that is a great friend!

~~~~~~

WHAT DOES GRIEF FEEL LIKE?

GRIEF IS EXPERIENCED UNIQUELY. I contemplated this question and came up with a list of ways grief feels to me. Please share your feelings of grief with me on my website: **lauriegrad.com** or on Twitter, **@lauriegrad**

➡ Grief is like living in a fog bank with no sunshine and only clouds. You cannot seem to focus enough to get through the mist and move out into the fresh air.

➡ Grief feels like an amputation. Your leg has been cut off, and you have to learn to walk again.

➡ Grief is like a deep wound that oozes and oozes until it finally begin to heal. Grief never really heals. It just leaves a permanent scar.

➡ Grief feels as if an elephant has landed on your chest. You can't get the weight off without shifting and turning, and you're trying to find your breath again.

➡ Grief is like being trapped in a bubble. You are isolated, with only muffled sounds from the outside that make no sense.

➡ Grief is like riding a roller coaster without a seat belt. You ride it to the top and then plummet to the bottom in seconds, fearing you will be tossed out into the atmosphere all alone.

➡ Grief is like the waves of the ocean, ebbing in and out and never stopping the cycle. Sometimes a wave of grief comes crashing down when you least expect it, and you feel swallowed up and unable to breathe.

➡ Grief feels like the world has turned to black and white and lost all color.

➡ Grief feels like nothing smells or tastes good anymore

➡ Grief is like landing on an alien planet where nobody speaks your language.

➡ Grief feels like part of your life has been erased.

➡ Grief is a constant feeling of disappointment, when you think your loved one is in the next room and then, to your horror, you remember he or she is gone.

➡ Grief is like being in the middle of a tornado that's twisting and tossing you around until you can find safe ground.

➡ Grief makes you feel like you are going mad.

➡ Grief makes you feel that you are all alone in the world.

➡ Grief feels as if you are burning up inside, and you can't find a fire extinguisher to stop the flames of pain.

➡ Grief is like trudging through thick mud that's slowing you down and making every step excruciating.

➡ Grief is like trying to figure out a puzzle that has no clues or answers.

➡ Grief is like a dull ache that never stops.

➡ Grief is like trying to swim upstream against a raging current where you think you are drowning.

➡ Grief is like living after the devastation of an earthquake. You find yourself sitting there, surrounded by the rubble that was once your life, and trying to find a way to put the pieces back together.

➡ Grief is like sitting on the sidelines of life. You watch it go forward, but you can't seem to find your focus or purpose for living.

➡ Grief is like being thrown into a bottomless pit, and you can't find a ladder to get out and up into the daylight.

➡ Grief is truly living a nightmare.

MEDITATION
Mindfully Trying to Move Forward

MY PERSONALITY DOESN'T COTTON to meditation. I know, I know, meditation and mindfulness would be excellent tools in my journey of grief, but in the early stages, I was too raw for it to work. I was afraid that the dams would open and the floodgates pour out a torrent of tears, but when a friend told me about a weekly free drop-in class called Mindful Awareness, offered by UCLA every Thursday at the Hammer Museum in Los Angeles, I decided to test the waters. The website described Mindful Awareness as "the moment-by-moment process of actively and openly observing one's physical, mental and emotional experiences. Mindfulness has scientific support that it can reduce stress, improve attention, boost the immune system, reduce emotional reactivity, and promote a general sense of health and well-being." It sounded acceptable for me, so I decided to go by myself.

I got a parking space in front of the building, an achievement in itself, and went inside. The doors of the museum were wide open. The ambience was airy and welcoming. I was directed to the Billy Wilder Theater, which had comfy seats, and I observed the legions of people streaming in. We're talking SRO! The late director Billy Wilder would have loved to have an SRO crowd at his movies and his namesake theater, even if it was just to relax. I noticed the diverse crowd, ranging from students to older people, all carrying backpacks, clad in jeans, ready to relax. I sat at the back of the room on the aisle with a planned escape route. I was very nervous about meditating, since my levels of concentration had been trashed by my grief. I was actually nervous about meditating mindfully!

An instructor from the UCLA Mindful Awareness Research Center sat down and began to talk in a comforting voice. She mentioned that it was holiday time and that we should focus on gratitude. At that point, my grief hit, and the tears spilled out onto my cheeks, dripping down in sheets of wetness. The thought of being grateful was difficult for me, but I forged ahead, tissues blotting my cheeks. She instructed us to breathe. This was really a problem because by then my nose was so stuffed that I was breathing through my mouth. I did not want to disturb the quietude with a loud honking nose blow, but I did so, and surprisingly I got a tender pat from my kind seatmate and her mother, which reassured me to continue.

The session was only twenty minutes longer, and I made it through, while dripping into my soaked tissues but continuing to try to find a focus. The gratitude issue kept popping up, and I tried to find a place in my heart to feel gratitude in my grief. I finally focused on my squad, my posse, my friends, and my family, who are there for me 24/7. I tried to repeat a mantra in my head: "Mindfulness is the gentle effort to be continuously present with experience. Mindfulness means paying attention to the present, without judgment." Even if all I could do was concentrate on my wet tissues, it was a small victory.

I got to my feet and was conscious of stares at my red nose and puffy eyes. My seatmate was ready to give me a hug. She was kind and sweet, and I left feeling spent but also proud of myself for attempting something beneficial on my own. It was progress.

A few months later, I attempted to try meditation again. My lovely niece Elizabeth Burrows has a fabulous studio in Manhattan called MNDFL, **mndflmeditation.com**, which I visited, and the concept seemed intriguing to me. She encouraged me to try meditation, a practice she felt could offer additional support for grief. She also cautioned that the effects of meditation are cumulative and that consistency is key, so it might take a while until I could calm my sorrows and let my breathing take hold. With grief, many of us hold on to unresolved issues with our loved ones. With Peter, nothing was left unsaid. I didn't need to ask for forgiveness or say good-bye. I just needed to find a way to resolve my deep yearning for him. I needed to empty out my backpack full of pain and hoped that meditation would be a start to finding some sort of analgesic.

To help me meditate, I signed up for an app called Headspace. The app is pretty user-friendly. It sets reminders on your calendar. It is certainly soothing to have a sexy Brit talking you through ten minutes of breathing a day. Headspace begins with a video of blue sky at the beginning of the series. The concept seems quite noble. They emphasize a strong appreciation for blue sky. They continue, "Sure, our view of the sky will be obscured by the clouds, but the clouds are temporary, fleeting, impermanent." OK, to sum up (always a reference from *The Princess Bride*): If I am to believe the concept of blue skies returning with confidence, I have to believe that my grief is impermanent and that I will once again part the clouds and find those skies of azure.

Mindfulness is at the core of Buddhist philosophy, and it is deeply connected to impermanence. If I were to value permanence, I would allow myself to look at the future obsessively or dwell in the past. That is *not* a good thing for a griever. If I accept impermanence, perhaps I can allow myself to live in the present moment, knowing that nothing lasts forever. Mindfulness reminds us that grief is impermanent. No, it won't go away completely. How could it? But if I can be mindful, maybe my grief will change shape and form and become more manageable in my new life. If I tell myself that my grief is not permanent, perhaps I can find small changes and victories that make me smile.

There is a tale of the Buddha that says he helped a woman who was trapped in her grief for her lost child, by asking her to collect a handful of mustard seeds, one from each home and family who had not experienced a death. The woman was unable to collect a single seed, as each and every family had a loss of its own. The lesson was intended to teach her the reality of death but, more importantly, to show how we are not alone in life. I like the philosophy that I am comforted by others, that my grief is not permanent, and that blue skies will return.

Despite all these plusses to meditation, I found that I was playing the Trivia Crack app to avoid hitting the Headspace button. Certainly, challenging my brain seemed a good excuse to put off relaxing, right? But I did forge ahead with my new Headspace app, and I even signed up for a year. I had a momentary meltdown the other day when the unknown British dude asked me to "discover the underlying sadness in my body." Ya think I have a touch of sadness in my body? But I continue each day, OK sometimes every few days, with my few minutes of Headspace, breathing and sobbing my way toward emptying my backpack of pain.

Other Thoughts:

➡ I have found that knitting is therapeutic and has a pleasant comforting effect, particularly if I am watching suspenseful television. I am not an advanced knitter, but I like the repetitive nature of the exercise as a calming technique.

➡ Deborah S. Derman, PhD, has come up with a coloring book called *Colors of Loss and Healing: An Adult Coloring Book for Getting Through Tough Times*, which other grievers find extremely consoling. I also enjoy reading the essays in *Healing After Loss: Daily Meditations for Working Through Grief*, by Martha Whitmore Hickman.

A few groaners for the road:

➡ "Meditation—You have the right to remain silent."

➡ "Don't just do something, sit there."

➡ "Life is hard. It's breathe, breathe, breathe, all the time."

CLEANING OUT THE CLOSET
When Is the Right Time?

AFTER PETER DIED I didn't think life could get any crueler, and then I realized that I had to face one of the worst, most gut-wrenching chores. I had to go through all his worldly possessions. This unbearable chore is on the very top of the stress meter of grief. Peter and I each had a closet in the bedroom, and after he died I would peer into his closet and weep uncontrollably. I nuzzled Peter's sweaters, I cuddled up into his cozy jackets, and I walked around in his extra-wide shoes, which was definitely a safety hazard since I have narrow feet. The pain of seeing the open closet just about killed me! (No pun intended.) I even shut the door and wept just at the site of the closed door. I had not yet realized and totally ingested the finality of Peter's death, and I was even having some "magical thinking" of keeping a few pieces in case he would come back. I recognized then and there that I had to go through his clothes and possessions so I could move forward in tackling my grief. I just knew the time was right to undertake this task.

I was keenly aware that I didn't want to do this alone. I needed moral, emotional, and physical support. The first step was to go through the mementos and jewelry and other keepsakes on his desk and in his closet. My son and his family helped since they wanted to keep many of these pieces as remembrances. Watches, rings, and pins were all distributed. I kept Peter's wonderful watch, which was a great comfort and which I still wear daily. The family and I also went through some of the clothes and put aside some pieces that would fit later on. Peter was a big guy, and not much would fit my son or grandson, but they each wanted some of Peter's possessions as remembrances.

A few days after Peter died, my close and caring friend and I brought garbage bags to the bathroom, and we tossed all the medicines, the toiletries, and even the shaving cream and razors, which I knew would be keen reminders of my loss. I was so grateful to have a friend help me get through this upsetting chore. I took a few breaks, but mainly I was focused on the word "declutter," which helped me to keep going.

Facing the closet set me off many times into wailing grief bursts, but I mustered all my courage to focus on the fact that Peter would want me to donate his clothes to help others. This became my closet mantra, and each time I cried, I kept thinking, "We are helping others." I had chosen to keep a few sweaters and some ties to remind me of Peter's scent and presence. Once I had done that, my amazingly empathetic friend offered to take over, and she organized for a charity to come and pack the clothes up and take them away while I hid downstairs at my computer. I donated to Beit T'Shuvah, **beittshuvah.org**, a wonderful organization that integrated integrated Jewish teachings, the twelve-step program for beating addiction, and the creative arts. Beit T'Shuvah believes everyone has the right to redemption, and practices never turning a single soul away due to their inability to pay. When the clothes were removed, I sensed that Peter and I were practicing T'Shuvah, meaning repentance and forgiveness, and having his death reap some positive meaning.

WHEN AND HOW TO GO THROUGH THE BELONGINGS

➡ Pace yourself and know when you are ready. There is no timetable that dictates when to go through the stuff.

➡ Know that getting rid of the belongings doesn't mean you get rid of grief. This odious chore is part of the process to help you heal.

➡ Focus on the fact that your loved one is here helping and would want you to donate to assist others in need.

➡ Tackle the project in steps, with lots of breaks. If you do it all at once, you will be exhausted.

➡ Make piles of things to toss out, things to donate to charity, and things that others might cherish.

➡ Remember no rash decisions! If you are not sure, hold on to an item for a while before discarding.

➡ Don't feel that you have to find the perfect home for each book or memento.

➡ If you want to store items in a storage unit, weigh the costs to you financially and emotionally.

➡ Don't hold on to any guilt about discarding stuff. You are helping the planet named Declutter.

➡ Start small. It becomes easier if you start tossing old socks and any clothes that are moldy or have holes.

➡ Tackle the desk and paperwork another time, when you are fresher.

➡ Do not let others judge you for how long or how short the time period is before you can tackle this heartrending task.

➡ Pat yourself on the back and celebrate the completion of this most difficult undertaking.

~~~~~~

A PERSON COULD DEVELOP A COLD
Sick and Alone

I LOATHE GETTING A cold. It only happens once or twice a year, but when I do get a cold, it goes right to my nose, and I can't smell or taste. As a foodie, my senses of smell and taste are my greatest pleasures. When I can't taste, I don't eat, and that is not a good thing for me. I have tried steaming in a shower. I have tried blowing my nose until I look like Rudolph! I have taken Mucinex (what an ugly name) but to no avail. I know that I just have to wait it out. It doesn't help that I cry at the drop of a hat at the thought of missing Peter, which adds extra snot to my already stuffed schnozzola. When Peter was alive and I was sick, he cajoled me with delicious food tidbits. He brought up bed trays of my favorite goodies, like soft scrambled eggs with crisp bacon, tuna sandwiches on well-toasted rye bread, or angel-hair pasta with butter and cheese. OK, he did make a mess in the kitchen, but I forgave him because his Florence Nightingale nursing skills were off the chart. He even ran to the garden to get a rose, which he put in a glass because he didn't know where the vases were. That was classic Peter, the kindest husband ever.

I recently got a whopper of a cold, and for the first time since Peter died, I had to minister to myself. I started sneezing in earnest and immediately ran to the market to get the fixings for chicken soup. My grandmother and mother made the best chicken soup on the planet and taught me just how it should taste. I begged the butcher for backs and necks, which have the best flavor since they have more bones and give extra health benefits. Once I secured the chicken parts, I ran around the market picking up onions, parsnips, carrots, celery with leaves, parsley, and from my Russian background, the secret ingredient, dill. I ran home before the cold overpowered me. I cooked the soup for two to three hours, while bingeing on Netflix! I strained the soup and kept the veggies to eat later. I discarded the chicken parts and then used a fat separator to remove all excess fat. It was a lot of work, I mean a lot of work, but then I had soup for this day and many to follow, and I stowed some in the freezer for a rainy day (although in LA, a rainy day is more of a wish).

CLASSIC CHICKEN SOUP
SERVES: 6–8

A classic chicken broth is prepared from a whole chicken, but it can be prepared from less expensive ingredients, such as chicken backs and necks. My mother taught me a few tricks to a clear, flavorful broth. First, the ingredients must be cooked at a slow simmer. If the soup boils too fast, it can become cloudy. The other trick is to use a little packaged or canned broth to start off the flavors.

6–7 pounds of chicken backs and necks or 1 5–6-pound chicken, rinsed well and cut into pieces (liver and giblets removed and saved for another use)

2 quarts water

4 cups defatted chicken broth (I prefer Whole Foods Chicken Stock, College Inn, or Swanson's Low-Sodium broth as a starter)

4 ribs celery, cut into 2-inch lengths, including the leaves

3 large carrots, peeled and cut into 2-inch lengths

3 large onions, peeled and quartered (keep a little of the brown skin for color in the soup)

3 large parsnips, peeled and cut into 2-inch lengths

2 large leeks, cleaned and cut into 1-inch lengths (white parts only)

3 sprigs fresh dill

3 sprigs fresh Italian parsley

8 peppercorns
2 whole cloves
1 bay leaf
    salt to taste
    Accompaniments: Wide noodles

1. Place the chicken parts, carrots, onions, celery, parsnip, and leeks in the bottom of a large, heavy, narrow stockpot. Place the dill, parsley, peppercorns, cloves, and bay leaf in a piece of cheesecloth, tie up with kitchen twine, and add to the pot with the salt.

2. Add the water and broth (the liquid should cover the chicken and vegetables completely) and bring to a boil; reduce the heat to medium-low, and allow the soup to simmer for 10 minutes, removing and discarding any scum that comes to the surface with a large spoon. Continue to cook the soup for 2½ to 3 hours, or until the flavors come together.

3. Allow the soup to cool slightly. Remove and discard the cheesecloth bag of herbs and spices, squeezing out any excess liquid into the soup. Remove the chicken and vegetables from the pot and save them for another use. Strain the clear soup into a container. Cool slightly, and then refrigerate the liquid so that the fat can be easily removed.

4. When ready to serve, remove the accumulated fat and reheat the soup. Add salt to taste, some noodles, the reserved chicken pieces, and serve hot.

～～～～～～～～～～～～～～～～～～～～

The chemistry of stress after a loss tells us that grief makes us susceptible to diseases such as the common cold, sore throats, and other infections. I know I have to eat right, exercise, get sleep (still hard), and talk about my emotions to relieve the stress. I know I should get massages and do all the right things. But sometimes, I just have to let chicken soup and rest do the trick!

To quote Miss Adelaide, in the show *Guys and Dolls*, which my father, the late playwright/director Abe Burrows wrote:

It says here:
The average unmarried female
Basically insecure

Due to some long frustration may react
With psychosomatic symptoms
Difficult to endure
Affecting the upper respiratory tract.
In other words, just from waiting around
for that plain little band of gold
A person can develop a cold.
You can spray her wherever you figure there's streptococci lurk
You can give her a shot for whatever's she's got,
but it just won't work
If she's tired of getting the fish eye from the hotel clerk
A person can develop a cold.

TO SLEEP, PERCHANCE TO DREAM
Sleeping Issues Dealing with Grief

I love sleep. My life has a tendency to
fall apart when I'm awake, you know?
—ERNEST HEMINGWAY

WHEN YOU ARE IN acute grief, drowsiness is a luxury. No matter how much I run around during the day, I can't get drowsy. I exercise daily just so I can have the comfort of fatigue. I go out at night with friends to delay getting into bed. I eye the clock as I watch TV. After 11:00 p.m., I turn off the lights, and the floodgates open. The reality of my new life, my solitude, my loneliness come crashing over me. I sob until there are no tears left. I even hope the crying will make me weary. Who knew that tiredness would become a luxury?

I am sad that I never cherished the rush of exhaustion that put me gently into slumber. Sleep has become elusive. I have tried drugs, drinks, and relaxation, but the art of enjoying that happy moment when my lids gently close is no longer available to me. I avoid caffeine; I don't take naps; I keep the room as cold as the tundra; yet sleep still eludes me. How much has changed on this journey of grief? Even the simplest parts of my daily existence have become an obstacle.

After Peter died I couldn't sleep on his side of the bed. He was a wonderfully big guy, and I can still feel the dent in the mattress where he slept. I even miss his snoring. Who knew I would give anything to hear those loud honking noises again? I sleep on my side only, and when I wake, I simply pull the corners up on the linens, and the bed is made. I don't thrash; I don't move about; I just stay in one corner of the big bed, wishing for rest.

Friends and family beg me to take care of myself. I eat well, I exercise, but at night, when the lights are out, my resolve to be good to myself is gone. My defenses are truly down. I revert to childlike stubbornness, and my will to fight in the dark ebbs. When will the anguish abate enough to allow for that blessed tiredness and release in the safety of sleep?

In the morning when I wake, the world comes into focus, and the realization of my new life becomes clear again. I used to love that extra time in bed in the morning when I would have another crack at cozy tiredness and those few minutes more of sleep until the alarm would wake me. Or I would snuggle into Peter's arms, and I would dream about facing the new day together. Instead I wake and start my distraction of a day hoping I can tire myself enough to feel the luxury of a soft sleep later that night. My pal Kath has taught me a game I will use. I think of people whose first and last names start with the same initials, like Abigail Adams, Benjamin Britten, and Charlie Chaplin. I find it soothing in a weird way to go down the alphabet. Does anyone know of a person with the initials XX?

SOME TIPS ON SOMNOLENCE

➡ A glass of wine is good to make you sleepy, but it doesn't provide a solid night's sleep.

➡ Cut way back on caffeine.

➡ Melatonin works for some, although it can wreak havoc with your body rhythms.

➡ Benadryl, which is in many over-the-counter sleep aids, works but often acts as a depressant or worse, leaves a hangover.

➡ Many swear by herbal sleep teas, but I have yet to find them helpful.

➡ Avoid naps during the day.

➡ Try using guided imagery, which is available on prerecorded audio programs.

➡ I know this is not PC, but please feel free to use a vibrator to relax before bed. It took me a while for me to use my vibrator after Peter died, but it has helped me immeasurably to relax.

➡ Do not go to sleep either when you are hungry, or after a heavy meal.

➡ Try taking a hot bath to relax.

➡ Try deep-breathing exercises in bed while imagining pleasing thoughts. This is tough at first, but as you move along on your grief journey, it will become easier.

➡ Exercise regularly, which helps to make you tired.

➡ Do not look at smartphones or tablets before bed. The blue light that LED screens give off can slow or halt the production of melatonin, the hormone that signals the brain that it's time for bed.

➡ Move to Alaska, California, Colorado, Maine, Massachusetts, Nevada, or any state that has legal weed!

~~~~~~

SAUDADE
The Presence of Absence

ON A RECENT TRIP to New York, I was fortunate to meet with Dr. Katherine Shear, Marion E. Kenworthy professor of psychiatry at the Columbia University School of Social Work. Dr. Shear works with those affected by complicated grief, which is defined by the Complicated Grief Center as "something getting in the way of adapting after the death of a loved one. When grief is complicated, the pain can be unrelenting and life seems empty of any possibility for happiness. We want to help lessen the pain. We want to make it possible to honor grief as a form of love." I was heartened to hear that I am not in complicated grief and that someone is addressing the problem for so many widows and widowers who can't move on.

I asked Dr. Shear many questions about grief, and she kindly gave me many nuggets of wisdom concerning grief therapy. I realize that reading book after book on grief is part of my process toward looking for answers. In my heart, I know there are no answers for getting through a loss such as mine, but in my head, I search feverishly for some miracle that will explain my pain. When she mentioned the word "saudade," I was intrigued enough to surf the Internet for its significance and the reason it gave me some degree of comfort.

"Saudade" is a Portuguese expression that is almost untranslatable. The best way to describe it is "the presence of absence." It is a longing for someone or something that you remember fondly but know you can never experience again. It is an awareness of the absence of a person or thing, which puts you in a deep emotional state of sadness. The presence of absence grapples with those who should be here but aren't. It is a form of homesickness and deep yearning. You are among thousands of people, but none is the one you want to be by your side. Saudade is the moment you realize the importance of the people in your life, and the moments you have taken for granted.

According to history, the word "saudade" came into being in the fifteenth century when Portuguese ships sailed to Africa and Asia. A sorrow was felt for those who departed for long journeys and who too often disappeared in shipwrecks or died in battle. Those who stayed behind deeply suffered from their absence. The survivors had a constant feeling that something was missing from their lives. The word is derived from the Latin plural "solitates," meaning solitudes, but it is also influenced by the word "salv," meaning safe. There is a dichotomy here between solitude and safety that I am trying to understand. I know the finite quality of loss, but the safe part of "saudade" is what inspires me. I miss Peter so deeply and want him by my side, and yet I am grateful for the moments I had with him. His absence is a presence in my soul and my heart that I will treasure forever.

Saudade is not nostalgia, where you reminisce about happy and sad emotions. You remember the happiness but feel the sadness, knowing you can't recapture the feeling. Nostalgia expresses a sensation one has for a loved one who has died, while saudade is the knowledge that Peter is absent from my life. Saudade provides comfort because, even in my sorrow, I sometimes feel an incongruous rush of joy in the hope of recovering something that will fill the presence of his absence.

> *Your absence has gone through me*
> *Like thread through a needle.*
> *Everything I do is stitched with its color.*
> —W. S. MERWIN, *SEPARATION*

FOR CRYING OUT LOUD
The Tracks of My Tears

I ADMIT TO OPENLY crying at movies and have even been known to cry at a commercial that includes a puppy. But I had no idea that I had so many tears in my body. I have cried so much since my sweet Peter died that I altered my vision and even improved my astigmatism! I have cried so much I could singlehandedly fix the California drought! I had no idea of the sadness that would befall me. I had no hint of the pain that would alter my existence. I had no inkling of the journey I would take in the path of grief. Just when I think I am a little bit better, the waves of sadness hit my brain and send a message to my tear ducts to start spilling.

I decided to do some research on tears. I discovered that there are three different kinds of tears. There are the basal tears that coat your eyes daily to keep them moisturized. The second type of tears are reflex tears, a.k.a. irritant tears, which form in response to pain, flush foreign objects out of the eye, or respond to scents like onions, and actually have some slight healing qualities. My overflowing-grief-type tears are the last type of tears, the emotional tears that well up in your eyes in response to feelings of sadness, stress, and even joy. I discovered that these tears have more protein-based hormones, including the neurotransmitter leucine enkephalin, which is a natural painkiller that is released when we are stressed.

When I have lunch or dinner with friends, the mere mention of Peter releases tears like a water fountain. My friends all hug me or hold my hand, and it makes us closer in a way that mere conversation could not facilitate. I am closer to friends through my tears and my raw emotions. I am beginning to believe that weeping is now a sign of courage, not weakness. If I am to understand that tears are helpful, then I will sob away, until I have the ability to make it through a day without tears.

I now have to address the practical portion of weeping. First, I have to tackle the puffy eyes. I have tried many products but have now zeroed in on Benefit's Puff Off!, which reduces swelling under the eyes. I was lucky enough to tattoo eyeliner on my eyes many years ago (man, did that hurt), so I don't have to worry about runny eyeliners and black eyes. I recently had eyelash extensions put on and now don't have to worry about mascara. If I did use mascara, the only one I would recommend is the totally waterproof Lancôme Définicils. So let the floodgates open and hope the healing begins. I hope to be able to be freely moved to tears, and know that it is good for me, especially since I have the practical measures under control.

To weep is to make less the depth of grief.
—SHAKESPEARE, *HENRY VI, PART II*

~~~~~~

ME, MYSELF, AND I
A Couple No More

One's not half of two; two are halves of one.
—E. E. CUMMINGS

THE DEFINITION OF THE word "couple" is "two persons married, engaged, or otherwise romantically paired." After forty-seven years of marriage, Peter and I would joyfully declare, "We are one." I gave Peter a key chain, which he kept throughout our marriage, with an inscription from E. E. Cummings that read, "We are so both and oneful." Our lives were wholly intertwined.

I now miss him every time I pass a photograph of him. I miss him every time I see a movie we treasured. I miss him while watching the finale of *Homeland* and am even sadder to miss him throw his shoe at the TV in frustration. I miss him when I am in the car and have to do all the driving. I miss him when I go to a restaurant and want him to sample my food even though he hated green veggies. I miss him in my bed, cuddling at night. I am all too aware that I am no longer a couple with two joined parts. I am single. I no longer have someone to share my innermost feelings and thoughts. I don't have a trusted partner as a confidant and a champion. I have lost the reflection of my love. Peter and I had a single language, a single sense of humor. But now I am single, without a sense of humor.

I used to look at single people with a smugness that I now regret. I would twirl my ring on my finger and stare at the symbol of my couplehood with pride. I didn't have to submit myself to online dating. I didn't have to find a friend to join me at the movies or theater. I didn't have to invite people to dinner. I had a live-in bestie, and we spent cozy nights together watching TV. Now that I am single, I feel unspeakably lonely. I find I feel envious of other couples as they march two by two, hand in hand, toward a phantom Noah's ark. Do I feel envious? Damn right I do! But deep down in my soul, I know that I have to find the strength to fill my life with my own form of entertainment and believe in the fact that I can find companionship and joy again, especially in my own company.

Mother Teresa talked honestly about loneliness. "The most terrible poverty is loneliness, and the feeling of being unloved." Loneliness is the hardest thing about grief. Loneliness is not the same as solitude or aloneness. Loneliness is a feeling of isolation, of disconnection from the rest of the world. Not only do I miss Peter, but I mourn the life we had as a couple. I miss making plans together for dinners, movies, and travel, and I even miss a walk into town. Yes, he hated exercise, but we would chatter along, and despite his protestations, he would feel great after. I feel the loneliness now because my life has been reduced to being internal. Who can share my life with me? The world is moving forward as couples stroll and hug and talk, and yet I am grieving still. Even being with family, I feel that I have lost a limb and can't heal.

I have decided not to plan too far in advance. The summer is looming large, but I can't even think about travel to faraway lands. I can't go down the road of the future, or it will make me sad. I have to live in the moment and, yes, be mindful of what is happening without looking ahead. When life hands you lemons, make lemonade—or at least Limoncello. I must find the power in myself to examine what kind of person I will become after this trauma. I have choices as a survivor of the hardest crisis to befall a human being, and I have to figure out how to reclaim my true self. I will go from widowhood to selfhood kicking and screaming but moving forward. I am still a mother, grandmother, sister, sister-in-law, and friend, but I am no longer a wife. I have to learn how to enjoy solitude. I don't have to lose my identity; I just have to find it again. The animals walked onto Noah's ark two by two.

I now have to find a way to be one by one or at least take steps to be kind to my one and only.

The worst loneliness is not to be comfortable with yourself.
—MARK TWAIN

~~~~~~

THIRD FINGER, LEFT HAND
That's Where He Placed the Wedding Band

'Cause he did something that no one else did
Friends said it couldn't be done
But all his love I know I've won'
Cause third finger, left hand
That's where he placed the wedding band.
—SUNG BY MARTHA AND THE VANDELLAS.
COMPOSED BY BRIAN HOLLAND,
EDDIE HOLLAND, LAMONT DOZIER

A WIDOW FACES A dilemma after her husband dies. She has worn a ring on the third finger of her left hand for her entire marriage. After he dies, she has to face the fact that not only is her life completely upended but now she is no longer married. It takes several months for this fact to fully sink in.

Historically it was once traditional for a widow to place her wedding ring in the casket with her husband, but thank goodness, this unseemly practice went by the wayside eons ago! Judith Martin, who writes the syndicated Miss Manners column, notes that the "Victorians' only rule for wedding rings worn by widows was that the ring should not be worn on the morning of a wedding to another man."

After Peter died, I would cry when I looked at my left hand. I was committed to Peter, and I didn't want that to end. I still used "we" when I talked about my life. There was no way I wanted to remove the symbol of our bond. I wasn't ready to accept the reality that I was alone and single. After about three months, I took the ring off. I don't know why, but it just felt right. I took Peter's ring, and all the rings he had given me, and bought a chain that I still wear, showing off my bling. I like that his ring sits over my heart and I feel his presence.

Most of my support-group members did similar things with their rings. Some put their husbands' rings on their right hands. Some wore them around their necks. Some just tucked them away in boxes. I discovered that there is no etiquette about when to remove your wedding ring. There is no right or wrong time. Some widows wear their rings forever. Some take them off immediately. There is no judgment about dealing with this representative symbol of your union. Just do what feels right for you. Take care of yourself and do what is good for you in your new single life.

REASONS TO KEEP WEARING YOUR WEDDING RING

➡ Your comfort level is fine with wearing it.

➡ You have zero interest in another relationship.

➡ You don't want to advertise that you are single and possibly get hit on.

➡ You enjoy wearing the ring as a symbol of your love.

➡ Looking at your ring gives you happy memories.

REASONS TO STOP WEARING YOUR WEDDING RING

➡ When you look at it, you feel sad and remember your loss.

➡ You are comfortable that you don't need a symbol to remember your lost love.

➡ You accept the reality that you are single and might be interested in dating.

ALTERNATIVE IDEAS OF WHAT TO DO
WITH YOUR WEDDING RING

➡ Wear your ring on a chain around your neck.

➡ Wear the ring on your right hand.

➡ Have the jeweler melt your ring and your spouse's ring into one ring that you can wear.

➡ Give the ring to your children or a loved one.

A YEAR OF NO
Just Say No!

SHONDA RHIMES PENNED A fabulous book called *A Year of Yes*, where she talks about being fearless enough to answer yes to new adventures. The loss of my sweet husband Peter has forced me to create my own version, "A Year of No." I have learned that in my journey of grief I have to be good to myself, and that means saying no. I have never been good at saying no, but I am perfecting this technique like a seasoned pro.

Now that I am giving the word no a chance, I have discovered there are various forms of no. There is the direct no, which I used recently. A friend asked me to chair a meeting for an organization while she was away. I was so surprised to hear a resounding no coming out of my mouth. She persisted, and I answered no again, and a third time too! It felt good. I know I am not up to being in charge. Perhaps one day I will be ready for the task, but for now, no is the best answer for me.

Then there is the meditative no, where you acknowledge the request but still decline. I was invited to a screening of a sad movie the other night. I replied that the movie sounded interesting but that I don't do sad movies at the present time. Give me a good Sandra Bullock movie and I am content. It just doesn't get better than *Miss Congeniality* for comfort.

How about the reasoned no? When asked if I would attend a big charity event or even a party, I replied that I was not ready to do this, and added that I might cry and break down as I did once before. I tell the hosts in the politest way possible that it is too hard for me now. This is a reasoned no. I have set reasonable boundaries gracefully.

There is also the mediator's no. If someone asks me to come to a party, I might reply, "I will come, but I might have to leave early." The mediator's no allows for negotiations, and the answer is on my own terms.

Right now, my favorite way is the delayed no. This is the safest way out of any situation. I simply answer an invitation by saying, "Sounds great, but I will let you know as soon as I have thought it over." This puts the ball back in my court, and I have time to think about saying no, or perhaps yes. Who knows?

The late Steve Jobs once said, "Focus is about saying no." That is my current mantra. I have to be a little bit selfish to help myself heal. I say no as respectfully as I can, knowing that my posse of good friends will understand.

No is a complete sentence.
It does not require justification or explanation.
—ANNE LAMOTT

A YEAR OF NO: WHEN "JUST SAY NO" IS A MUST!

➡ The direct no: "Thanks but no thanks."

➡ The meditative no: "I might come, but I have to weigh my options."

➡ The reasoned no: "I am not ready to do anything yet."

➡ The mediator's no: "I will come but I might have to leave early."

➡ The delayed no: "Sounds great but I will let you know as soon as I have thought it over."

BAH HUMBUG
A Year of Firsts, Holidays, and Marker Dates

I AM STEELING MYSELF against the upcoming holidays. Each mile-stone is a weight that I carry. I feel like Sisyphus in Greek mythology, being punished and forced to roll an immense boulder up a hill only to watch it roll down for all eternity. That is the ups and downs of grief. You have to get the boulder up the mountain, not sure whether it will stay there, or put me back into a state of pain again.

The anticipation of Thanksgiving is bad enough, but I feel this tremendous burden of having to go through the day without turning into a blubbery mess. Thanksgiving is so family oriented. Peter used to love to go to his sister's wonderful dinner. He adored eating the delicious turkey and stuffing, and he enjoyed all the traditions surrounding it. Let's face it: he loved to eat, and this is a favorite holiday for fressers, those who love to eat. The holiday season was also about the Raiders! We wore silver and black whenever they played. Peter screamed at the TV, and my son and grandson delighted in his enthusiasm for a team that never really won.

Thanksgiving makes us analyze the word "gratitude." It is hard for a griever to be thankful or grateful when they have experienced such a profound loss. You might hear someone say, "be grateful for the time you had together." Nothing feels worse to someone in grief than this comment! But if you analyze the word gratitude, and find just a scintilla of pleasure in a funny movie, a good day without sobbing, or just a moment of peace, you can begin to see gratitude the way the word was intended. Gratitude is not about comparing or contrasting; it is about cherishing one moment of pleasure in the many moments of pain.

Thanksgiving is the first big holiday I will experience as a widow, and it brings up the year of the firsts. I will have my first Chanukah, Christmas, New Year's Eve, our anniversary, his birthday, and finally my birthday. How the hell will I get through all of these in one piece? The very thought turns my stomach.

Holiday times evoke the pleasure Peter and I had giving gifts to the grandkids. We trolled the aisles of Costco on our early Sunday jaunts and looked for fun gifts that they would love. Speaking of Costco, Peter couldn't wait for the cashmere sweaters to arrive, and he would buy them for his nephews, who didn't wear sweaters or even like cashmere. But it was a Peter Grad tradition, which I will miss, even though cashmere is too hot for Southern California!

Peter and I always had a no-gift policy. He would ignore this declaration and immediately visit my favorite jewelry store to pick out something a little too sparkly. Then we would return it together, and I would get something I liked. I would get him a sweater from his favorite store, which he would try on, and then we would go back to his favorite store and return it. This was our tradition, and I will miss it. I will miss it and miss him even more than I can express.

Then I remember that I can't live in the future while I grieve. I have to live in the present. I have to live one second at a time. I can prepare for the pain of the holidays, but I can't go down the road too far because if I do, the boulder will fall down again, and I cannot focus on healing in the present.

I have decided to have a plan B in place. In case Thanksgiving is too hard, I will go home and watch a movie and sob into a bowl of popcorn. I could also not go and really feel sorry for myself, but I scrap that plan since I want to be with my family. Whatever I do, I know that I am not being selfish; I am just caring for myself.

The holidays will never be the same joyous experiences. But I have to believe, in some part of my being, that I will find a new way of celebrating. Recovery from loss is achieved by a series of small and hopefully correct choices, so I will take small steps forward even if I have to fall back a few times. The one constant I have is my friends, whom I have been calling my posse. They listen, they nurture, and they keep me going. My grandson says I should call them my squad. I looked up "squad" online, and the definition is "a crew, posse, gang: an informal group of individuals with a common identity and a sense of solidarity." That sounds like just the support team I need. So I dedicate this quote from Cole Porter, in his wonderful song "Friendship," to my squad:

If you ever lose your mind, I'll be kind

And if you ever lose your shirt, I'll be hurt

If you're ever in a mill and get sawed in half

I won't laugh

It's friendship, friendship, just a perfect blend ship

When other friendships are up the crick.

Ours will still be slick!

LAURIE'S HOLIDAY SURVIVAL TIPS

➡ Take care of yourself: get enough sleep and exercise.

➡ Indulge! 'Tis the season, so allow yourself small holiday treats, such as comfort foods like pumpkin pie and lots of eggnog! One caveat: don't eat a quart of ice cream alone! The cold will feel good going down but won't feel good in the morning.

➡ If it is not too painful, make a toast to your loved one to honor your relationship.

➡ Give yourself permission to be honest with family and friends about how you feel! If you don't feel grateful this year, your friends will understand.

➡ Discover ways to have enjoyment while taking good care of yourself. Take a hike, visit with friends, or just curl up with a blanket and binge-watch Netflix.

➡ Remember that you have the right to say "time out" any time you need.

➡ Get out of town. It might be easier to avoid
   Thanksgiving or Christmas by traveling with
   a pal on your first holiday alone.

➡ Be around positive people that make you happy.
   It is better to be alone than with people who make
   you feel worse!

➡ Do it your way. Plan Ahead. If that means having
   a plan B escape strategy, then by all means set it up.

➡ Stay away from social media. Seeing all those
   families together will compound your own loss.

DINNER FOR ONE
Feeding Yourself Royally

IN THE MONTHS SINCE Peter died, I have been eating out much of the time. Ever since I wrote "Demoted to Lunch," my friends have listened and begun treating me to dinners nonstop. Now that things have quieted down, I seem to have more time at home in the evenings, and my dinners are downright pathetic! Trader Joe's quinoa and veggies (the best choice of this list), baked potato with butter and cheese, biscuits with butter, scrambled eggs, and even raisin bran! This might seem normal for a new widow, but I am a food writer by trade! I should know better than to eat nothing but carbs. I have penned four cookbooks, have had my own cooking show on The Learning Channel, and write for a website about cookbooks and cookware each month!

I knew I had to turn things around. I started to do a few dinner parties to pay people back for their hospitality. This was particularly hard when I set the table for eight and then dissolved in a puddle knowing we were only seven. But my menu inspired me to continue. I served gravlax with mustard dill sauce, my famous recipe for rack of lamb with grainy mustard sauce (thank you, Costco, for the most fabulous lamb), roasted baby potatoes and cipollini onions with rosemary, a composed salad, and sticky toffee pudding for dessert. This particular meal is easy to prepare, but I have whipped it up three or four times and have to get my creative juices flowing (forgive the pun).

I may have been able to organize a few dinner parties, but my own eating habits in the last few months have been pretty pathetic and not very healthful—this from a woman who taught "Light and Easy Cooking" on television! I had to formulate a plan for cooking for one. I had the skills, I had the recipes, and my pantry was stocked with all the right foods, but I just didn't have the motivation. Then one day I began to crave chili. I have a great turkey-chili recipe in my last cookbook, and I suddenly had the urge to start cooking. I wrote this recipe for Peter since he hated beans and felt that cilantro was the antichrist. I decided to make it with lots of beans. Now that I sleep alone, I don't have to worry about the aftereffects of beans. I can still see Peter laughing at the farting scene from *Blazing Saddles*. I chose to double the recipe and have enough in my freezer for several meals. Once inspired, I decided to also make a vegetable soup I love called Tuscan ribollita. I went to the farmers' market and loaded up on lots of veggies, ran to my local market to get my chili ingredients, and set aside a morning to cook. I turned on the score of *Hamilton* and started to chop, sauté, and enjoy myself in the kitchen while listening to Lin-Manuel Miranda rapping history.

My chili was delicious, and I paired the dish with a lovely red wine (from Costco of course). I put out sour cream, grated cheese, avocado, and copious amounts of cilantro. It wasn't a silver lining, but it was a change. I enjoyed my dinner, although I was watching *Masterpiece Mystery* at the time. Small steps. At least I cooked my own TV dinner!

TURKEY CHILI WITHOUT BEANS
SERVES: 8–10

Traditionally, chili is prepared with chopped meat and served with beans on the side. My sweet Peter hated beans, so I created this recipe for his tastes. This version integrates today's lighter eating habits by using ground turkey instead of beef and oil instead of butter or lard. I ask the butcher to grind turkey thighs especially for chili, which is a chunkier mixture.

If you prefer chili with beans, add 2 15-ounce cans of rinsed and drained beans and bake the cooked chili in a covered pot in a 325° oven for about 30 to 40 minutes until heated through.

> **2** tablespoons olive oil
> **2** large onions, chopped

4 large garlic cloves, minced
2 pounds lean ground turkey, chopped for chili
¼ cup chili powder
1 tablespoon ground cumin
2 teaspoons dried oregano, crumbled
2 teaspoons unsweetened cocoa powder
½ teaspoon cayenne powder or to taste
  salt and freshly ground pepper to taste salt to taste
1 28-ounce can crushed-fire-roasted-tomatoes packed
  in purée
1 12-ounce bottle dark beer
½ cup defatted chicken broth
1 bay leaf
  Accompaniments: warmed corn tortillas, diced
  avocado, salsa, grated sharp cheddar cheese,
  chopped onions, chopped cilantro, chopped
  tomatoes, and sour cream or yogurt.

1. Heat 1 tablespoon of the oil in a large nonstick Dutch oven, or similar-sized nonstick pan, and when hot, cook the turkey, chopping and separating with a spoon, until it loses its pink color, about 5 or 6 minutes. Drain the meat into a colander to remove the excess fat and liquid, and set aside.
2. Increase the heat to high, add the remaining 1 tablespoon of the oil and sauté the onions, stirring often, for about 5 or 6 minutes, until softened. Add the garlic and stir just to combine, about 30 seconds.
3. Add the chili powder, cumin, oregano, cocoa powder, cayenne, and salt; reduce the heat, and continue to cook for an additional 2 minutes over moderately high heat to incorporate the spices. Add the drained turkey, tomatoes, beer, broth, and bay leaf; bring to a boil, reduce the heat, cover, and simmer for 30 minutes, stirring occasionally. Remove the cover and continue to cook until thickened. Remove and discard the bay leaf.
4. Serve the chili hot with any or all of the following toppings: warmed corn tortillas, diced avocado, salsa, grated sharp cheddar cheese, chopped onions, chopped cilantro, chopped tomatoes, and sour cream or yogurt.

WHAT YOU NEED TO KNOW ABOUT GRIEF
What to Expect When the Unexpected Happens

I HAVE LEARNED THAT grief is a natural process, not a disease from which you recover. Grief is the normal human response to a substantial loss. Grief is also decidedly unique. All people will grieve on their own terms, and in their own timetable. Understanding the process of grief and knowing what to expect will help you cope. The pain will still be there, but somehow hearing the following can be extraordinarily soothing and comforting for grievers:

➡ The worst kind of grief is yours! When you lose a significant person in your life, it hurts, and nothing takes away your right to totally feel that loss and grieve deeply.

➡ Grief is all powerful. It will catch you unprepared, even if it is expected. Grief reminds us of the fragility of life and our own vulnerability.

➡ Everyone grieves uniquely. Age, gender, culture, and personality all affect how one grieves.

➡ Grief work is probably the hardest work you will ever do. It requires intense physical and emotional energy to work through the pain. Grief work gets trickier when misconstrued expectations of strength hinder our process.

➡ The way out of grief is to face it head on. There is no

easy end run around the process. There are no short-
cuts or easy passes through grief. You must muster the
courage and face the pain head on to find your new
normal. To quote Helen Keller, "The only way to get
to the other side is to go through the door."

➡ Grief requires infinite patience. The way you feel
immediately after the death and the months that
follow will change drastically. Learn to practice
self-compassion to help you through the process.

➡ Successful grieving is not done alone. Many people
believe grief is so personal, we want to shut ourselves off. Finding a person to listen without
judgment is key. Sharing experiences in a support
group is invaluable.

➡ Be assertive and learn to say no to take care of
yourself. Don't be afraid to ask for what you need.

➡ Talk all you want! Cry all you want!

➡ Don't worry about what others think. Grief is not
a competitive sport!

➡ Your grief will take longer than you think. Grieving
is a lifelong process. While the initial intense pain
dulls over time, it never completely disappears from
your life. Grief is like a deep wound that builds up
scar tissue and heals slowly, but you will always feel
some of the pain.

➡ Grief may include secondary losses, like financial
security, status, and your dream future, which can
all be devastating.

➡ It is not the passage of time that heals grief; it is
what you do with that time that matters. If you use
your time wisely and grieve actively, you will learn
to bounce forward.

➡ Your relationship with your loved one doesn't
end with death. The bond you had will endure in
your heart. Find new ways to relate to your loved
one by establishing new rituals to commemorate
the memory.

THE JOKE'S OVER; YOU CAN COME BACK NOW
Laurie's Mourner's Bill of Rights

AT LEAST ONCE A day I look for Peter. I look when I put my key in the lock and open the front door. I look when I have gotten into bed and wait for him to slip under the covers beside me. I look when I go downstairs to his office. I look when I sit at my desk, waiting for him to come to the kitchen and sneak a cookie. His presence is in the house, in the pictures, in the books, in the furniture, in the very soul of our home. It has been over half a year since Peter died, and on some level, I still believe I will see him walk in the door and tell me, "The joke's over; I'm back."

Then reality sinks in, and I remember I am alone and have to learn to share my thoughts with myself as my new sounding board. I have to learn to watch television on my own and comment to myself about how bad the Golden Globes were this year; about how good *The People v. O. J. Simpson* is; about the lunacy of Donald Trump (even though it seems we were at the University of Pennsylvania at the same time); and about how much better *Project Runway Junior* is than regular *Project Runway*.

I have to drive myself to parties—with an occasional Uber. With the help of Audible.com, I can even drive to Malibu engrossed in a historical bodice ripper; a Broadway theatre exposé like *Razzle Dazzle*; or a gripping novel like *Fates and Furies*, which was so good I stayed in my driveway for half an hour just to finish it.

Humans are like herd animals. We don't do well alone. We need to feel secure. With sudden death, we are thrown back to an earlier time, when we were children groping with finding our own personalities.

In loss, we are like weak little children again, looking for our own selves to blossom. So now I must learn to find that child in me and help her to grow up emotionally and practically. I must learn to uncork champagne bottles, open stuck windows, find the fuse box in a power outage, handle finances, and most importantly make decisions on my own.

So, I have devised my own Mourner's Bill of Rights to help me cope with learning to be content with living solo.

LAURIE'S MOURNER'S BILL OF RIGHTS

➡ I have the right to mourn on my own timeline.

➡ I have the right to discuss my grief ad nauseam.

➡ I have the right to hide pictures until I am ready to accept the memories.

➡ I have the right to retail therapy.

➡ I have the right *not* to be a model griever.

➡ I have the right to tell people who say platitudes, to take a hike.

➡ I have the right to say no to a party.

➡ I have the right to cry at any time or place as long as tissues are within reach.

➡ I have the right to take my anger out on telemarketers.

➡ And I have the right to eat ice cream for dinner!

~~~~~~~~~~~~~~~~~~~~~~~~~~~~~~~~

THE COMFORTING ARMS OF A SUPPORT GROUP

WHEN PETER DIED, I openly welcomed all the help I could get. I went to a grief therapist and learned tools for coping with the daily onslaught of bottomless and relentless pain. I learned to find solace in the support of my friends and family, and accepted their cradling arms and nurturing words of "we got your back."

But I knew I needed more support, and was lucky enough to find a haven at the amazing Our House Grief Support Center, **ourhouse-grief.org**. I intuitively understood that one-on-one grief therapy was good but that a group would be a safe haven to find solace, companionship, and a shared sense of understanding. I had read a great deal about groups, and I knew that Our House had totally affordable grief support groups that were specific to the age of the griever, the length of time since the death, and most importantly, the relationship between griever and loved one. Each of us in the group had endured the death of a beloved spouse. The center also supports grieving children, teens, and adults, and has available groups in Spanish as well.

The group bonded from the day we began. Family and friends can help you to a point. A group gets it. Once we told our stories, we found a mutual and tacit understanding of our loss. We were like-minded folks hoping that our shared pain and permission to grieve openly (buoyed by many tissue boxes in abundance all over the room) would take us through our journey. We were not all the same age, but we shared our hearts, and our hearts were healed as a group. I am sure everyone feels his or her group is special, but I have a special kinship to my peeps, who called me "Miss Sassy" because I pretty much would say anything and openly talk about my *tsuris* (Yiddish for troubles, tribulations, and suffering). The group was a safe sounding board for us to frankly share our deepest angst and pain. I will forever be grateful to my group members for carrying me through the tough times and transporting us all through the tunnel of grief and out into the light of the possibility of new life.

There were ten when we started, but we shrank to six key and vocal members with two fantastic leaders who helped guide us across the stepping stones on the path toward finding our new lives. Our caring facilitators took us through exercises, journaling, and places we were afraid to tread, so that we could face the world again. Some members had experienced sudden deaths like I did, but others had slower more lingering deaths. It didn't matter. We were all in the same bottomless-pit-of-a-boat, sailing through winds and storms of pain, which we navigated together. No one stopped us from crying. The leaders didn't offer us tissues because no one should offer a tissue that might inhibit the freedom to cry. Instead we offered hugs, and embracing arms, and tissues to each other, when each of us dared to reveal our innermost thoughts.

Being in a support group is empowering because you learn you are not alone. Others have gone before you, and others will follow you, but grief support groups assist by helping you to come together and move on from an isolated view of pain into a collective goal toward healing. My group shared coping techniques, we never judged one another, and we exchanged thoughts and ideas that mutually benefitted our recovery. Sure, the exercises were disgustingly wrenching, especially when we wrote letters to our loved ones, but it all made sense when we graduated after an eighteen-month commitment, and we knew that we would always somehow be in each other's lives in some capacity in the future. We had shared the worst emotional pain of our lives, and that combined emotion kept us forging forward and attempting to discover some kind of joy in life.

THE BENEFITS OF A SUPPORT GROUP

➡ To give emotional support to those grieving in a safe and nonjudgmental environment.

➡ To be with others who have experienced a similar loss and truly get what you are going through.

➡ To provide a safe place to tell your story and begin the healing process.

➡ To furnish a protected atmosphere in which you have permission to grieve openly and speak freely about your loss.

➡ To teach you coping skills to help on your journey through grief.

➡ To provide a place to experience shared companionship and know that you are not isolated and alone in your pain.

HOW TO SELECT A SUPPORT GROUP

➡ Geographic location should be a big factor. You want to be close by so you are not stressed even further with long commutes.

➡ The center should offer peer group therapy.

➡ You should be with others who are in the same time frame as you. It is important to go through group with those who are at the same state of recovery.

➡ Consider age appropriateness. It is important to be with people near your age. The first group I was in, I was with people twenty years older, who didn't get me. Then I joined a younger group and bonded.

➡ Consider the type of loss. It is necessary to be with people who have similar losses, like the death of a spouse, child, or parent.

THE BEST READS FOR A WIDOW
Bibliotherapy

AFTER PETER DIED, I became obsessed with books on grief, voraciously reading everything I could get my hands on. I was looking for answers, but in grief, there are no answers; there is only a long, slow process of adaptation to a new life alone. I found comfort turning the pages and using my highlighter and sticky notes to mark each passage that resonated with my experience. Reading yielded benefits for me. I didn't feel as isolated when I read that others were going through the same wrenching journey. Comprehending the words others penned made me feel reassured and validated in my own angst. As I learned more about grief, I felt that I was doing the right R & D to help get me through the tough times. Each book offered a bit more enlightenment and education, which further helped me forge ahead on my trek through grief.

Memoirs were tougher to get through than the self-help books, but they were also quite cathartic, resonating with my own experience. You would think that while in the midst of your own grief, reading someone else's memoir would be the last thing that would help. But knowing that others had been there before me, and lived to tell the tale, seemed to normalize my grief process. Each book brought another aspect that rang true, and that knowledge helped with my self-esteem, knowing that there were others who had been down the road and survived.

Binge reading is a healthy vice. It certainly beats the numbing qualities of booze and drugs. Gleaning knowledge from others who have trod before you can arm you with the tools to continue on. You feel smarter and more knowledgeable, and ergo, you can become a more empathetic and understanding person.

Amazingly, there is a name for reading as a tool to survive tough times: bibliotherapy. Bibliotherapy is a creative therapy that involves the reading of specific texts with the purpose of healing. At the School of Life in London, you can actually have a bibliotherapist write you a book "prescription" for whatever is bothering you.

Below please find my prescription for books that helped me immeasurably and hopefully will help you through your journey through grief:

LAURIE'S SUGGESTED GRIEF READING LIST

Healing after Loss: Daily Meditations for Working Through Grief, by Martha Whitmore Hickman

Grief One Day at a Time: 365 Meditations to Help You Heal After Loss, by Alan D. Wolfelt, PhD

Healing a Spouse's Grieving Heart: 100 Practical Ideas after Your Husband or Wife Dies, by Alan D. Wolfelt, PhD

A Widow's Guide to Healing: Gentle Support and Advice for the First 5 Years, by Kristin Meekhof, LMSW, and James Windell, MA

Life after Loss: A Practical Guide to Renewing Your Life after Experiencing Major Loss, by Bob Deits, M. Th.

The Year of Magical Thinking, by Joan Didion

On My Own, by Diane Rehm

A Time to Grieve: Meditations for Healing after the Death of a Loved One, by Carol Staudacher

Healing Grief, Finding Peace: 101 Ways to Cope with the Death of Your Loved One, by Louis E. Lagrand

Widow to Widow: Thoughtful, Practical Ideas for Rebuilding Your Life, by Genevieve Davis Ginsburg, MS

The Heart of Grief: Death and the Search for Lasting Love, by Thomas Attig

Option B: Facing Adversity, Building Resilience, and Finding Joy, by Sheryl Sandberg and Adam Grant

Resilient Grieving: Finding Strength and Embracing Life after a Loss That Changes Everything, by Lucy Hone, PhD

When a Spouse Dies: What I Didn't Know about Helping Myself and Others Through Grief, by Barbara R. Wheeler, DSW

Understanding Your Grief: Ten Essential Touchstones for Finding Hope and Healing Your Heart, by Alan D. Wolfelt, PhD

Living with Loss, One Day at a Time, by Rachel Blythe Kodanaz

MEMORIES—MISTY WATER-COLORED MEMORIES OF THE WAY WE WERE
Looking At Pictures Can Be Difficult

FOR THE PAST FEW months, I have received an e-mail of my "daily memory updates" on Facebook. Every time the e-mail came in, I would quickly delete it because there would be a picture of Peter and me traveling, cozying up with the family, or having fun with friends. Suddenly I realized I could stop the daily pictures and reminders, which were way too painful. I have lost my partner with whom I shared memories. I want to laugh about funny memories. I want to bring back some fond times, but I am definitely not ready at this time.

I am keenly aware that I have to make new memories with my family, especially those amazing grandkids. I have talked to widows and widowers who all have different views on this subject. Some like to keep the pictures in view, and look at them daily. Some, like myself, put the pictures away until we can face them in a better frame of mind (stop with the puns, Laurie!). I don't know when that will be, but I hope it will be soon because he was the most handsome man, and what a head of hair! Men in their twenties were jealous of Peter's mane.

Right after Peter died, I suddenly realized that I had to change my ICE (in case of emergency) contact. I quickly entered all the information for my son as my new primary ICE contact. I love my son dearly, but the wave of emotion that overcame me when I had to delete Peter's contact was devastating. I still measure time by **BPD** (before Peter died) and **APD** (after Peter died). I know that one day all the pictures and memories will be touching and soothing, but right now I am still in intense grief, and I have to utilize the Pause button until I am ready.

The other thing I discuss with my therapist, and in my group, is what to do with the ashes. The ashes were shipped to me by Priority Mail from Colorado, where he died. Who knew that you are not allowed to ship ashes by FedEx or UPS? I put him in our gym, but not on the treadmill because Peter hated to work out. I put him in a cabinet under the television, where he would be content. We had talked about being scattered together perhaps on our favorite spot on the beach in Montecito. But Peter had always requested that his ashes to be scattered on the fourteenth green at Cypress Point Golf Club because "there has never been a Jew who is a member." A friend took a small scoop of Peter's ashes up to Monterey and scattered them across the road from the hole. In a second, a gust of wind came by and scattered the ashes right on the fourteenth green! I am so glad that I got to grant him his wish.

Eight months after Peter died, I decided to honor his memory at the benefit we chaired for the Alzheimer's Association for twenty-four years. It was so satisfying to work together to raise money for this amazing organization, memorializing my father's descent into the depths of Alzheimer's disease. It was a passion for both of us, and Peter worked tirelessly to raise funds. I knew that it would be a difficult night, but I also knew I had to honor his work and his memory in the way he would have appreciated. The love in the room, and the support I felt, made Peter's memory soar in my heart. This was the way I wanted to remember my love and the way he would have loved to be remembered.

Memories may be beautiful and yet
What's too painful to remember we simply choose to forget
So it's the laughter we will remember
Whenever we remember the way we were.
—MARVIN HAMLISCH

DEATH OF A SOUL MATE
The Gut-Wrenching Loss of a Spouse

He felt now that he was not simply close to her,
but that he did not know where he ended and she began.
—LEO TOLSTOY

THE TERM "SOUL MATE" dates all the way back to Plato. It is a generic word for a close loved one. But the phrase "soul mate" itself was first recorded in 1822, when the poet Samuel Taylor Coleridge wrote in a letter, "To be happy in Married Life…you must have a Soul-mate." In today's vernacular, the word "soul mate" has come to connote a much more intimate nature. A soul mate today means a more mystical commingling of heart and soul into a "twin flame," destined to be together for eternity.

Peter and I always felt we were each other's missing half. It was as if we were pieces of a puzzle that had come together and fit perfectly. Peter was the mirror to my soul. He was my cheerleader. He wanted me to succeed, and I, in turn, wanted him to flourish. We were one organism that functioned as an integrated unit. He was the key to my lock, and I gave him the key to my chastity belt. (I had to inject some humor since the tears were wetting my keyboard.) We felt safe in our love, and we allowed each other to function at a level of honesty and honor without pretenses. We attained a level of comfort and security that gave us a safety net that not many couples share. We were inseparable companions, enjoying our daily rituals of check-in phone calls and texts and anticipating when we would be home to share stories of our day. They were our verbal ablutions, and we cherished them to the max. We desperately wanted to grow old together and keep our life rhythm pulsing. We both felt privileged to have shared such a rare intimacy and kindness toward each other. We felt grateful to share a sense of humor and perseverance about life. We were truly soul mates.

It is said to lose a parent is to lose the past. To lose a child is to lose the future. To lose a spouse is to lose the present. I feel as if I have been robbed. Something irreplaceably valuable has been stolen from me. I have lost my present with the death of my soul mate, and the grief is dreadfully painful. I feel as if a limb has been amputated. Part of me has been torn away, and I am flailing to find a sense of equilibrium and right myself to move forward without crashing. It is the most heart-wrenching experience of my life, and by the nature of its overwhelming power, it has made me question whether I want to go on. The hardest part about a loved one dying is not that the person is gone but that you are still here. The dilemma of losing a part of you is that your relationship has been abruptly severed, and you are left to sift through the emotional debris and extract your self from your missing coupledom.

My grief is a byproduct of the intense love I shared with Peter. We were lucky to have found each other and shared a whole lifetime together. To quote Jule Styne in his musical *Funny Girl*:

> *Lovers are very special people.*
> *They're the luckiest people in the world.*
> *With one person, one very special person.*
> *A feeling deep in your soul,*
> *Says you are half now you're whole.*
> *No more hunger and thirst,*
> *But first be a person who needs people.*
> *People who need people,*
> *Are the luckiest people in the world.*

After Peter died, I felt that my whole was diminished to half. My other half, my better half, was suddenly gone, and part of something attached to me had died too. The couple that we were, was completely gone. I had to decide if my life was now half empty or half full. In the beginning, I was emptied of all feeling. I was mourning the couple we had been and the empty half I had become. I was insecure in my decisions. My confidence was shot, and I felt inadequate to face the future. I lost my unconditional best friend and partner who shared my convictions and my feelings. I was bereft of that champion, and I flailed around for many months in insecurity and self-doubt.

But as time moved on, I knew I had to restore my view to believe "my life is half full, not half empty." I hoped that if I changed my attitude to see my life as half full, I could begin filling up the half of my life that was unfulfilled. It gave me the room for expansion and growth so I could look toward a new beginning in my life. I knew that I had to relearn how to live without Peter; I had to relearn the meaning of life, which had been shattered with his death; and I had to relearn how to love him in absentia.

I began to assess my attributes and take stock of the inventory of my soul. I strove to find the best me that I could so that I could become whole in my own company. I had to stop swooning at the Hollywood sentiment in *Jerry McGuire's* "You complete me!" Peter and I did complete each other. I had to turn this phrase upside down and find the real me who would be enough to satisfy and complete me on my own.

For the sake of my family and friends, I must find a life without Peter. I must find a safe haven through my mourning process. Mourning is the driving force that makes the journey of grief move forward. I vow to remain in the pain of grief long enough, but not a day longer than necessary. But I also vow to stay in the process of grief for not a day less than I need. The only way I can adapt to my new life is to heal from the inside out.

~~~~~~

HOW TO COPE WITH GRIEF BURSTS

GRIEF BURSTS, ALSO REFERRED to as "sudden temporary upsurges of grief" (STUG), are the swells of grief triggered by a song, a location, a scent, an anniversary, a birthday, a holiday, a photograph, or a memory of a loved one. These grief bursts are a normal part of the journey through grief, helping you to acknowledge the reality of life without your loved one. For me, it can be the smell of a Dunkin' Donut, Peter's absolute favorite, that puts me into a puddle of snot and tissues. Sometimes it is a song, or a glance at his cute face with that beautiful head of hair in a photo. Sometimes, grief bursts come out of the blue in the shower when I'm just staring at his soap. At first, I couldn't pass a hoagie shop (another one of Peter's vices) without sobbing. It seemed that grief demanded my full and complete attention. Little by little the grief bursts eased up so that they only hit once every few days when I was down or haunted by too much TV news!

Each time a grief attack happens, you come to understand your grief a little better. As you learn about your grief, you assess which are the provocative sparks, and avoid the minefields of those triggers. I don't like grief, but I have learned that I have to work with grief as my partner, in order to discover what life offers me in my new solo existence.

Grief bursts are normal and provide a great release, but they often catch you off guard. Here are a few ways to protect yourself:

> ➡ Avoid sad movies, especially about death. Stick with comedy, comedy, comedy!

➡ If you think you will be hit by a STUG (sudden temporary upsurge of grief) while watching an instant tearjerker television show such as *This Is Us*, watch a good sitcom instead. After two years, I am enjoying *This Is Us*, and I am able to cry without being catapulted into a grief burst.

➡ If you are listening to audible books, make sure they are upbeat. You don't want a grief burst in the car. If you have one, be smart: pull over until it subsides!

➡ Label a STUG a STUG. Knowing that it is a normal part of grieving and will not last, diminishes its power. Remember the word "temporary" in the acronym STUG!

➡ Think of a STUG as a tribute to your loved one, and a reminder that love never dies but lives on in your heart.

THE VULTURES ARE CIRCLING
How Low Can You Go?

JUST AFTER PETER DIED, my accountant warned me about being scammed. I thought I was pretty savvy, and assured him, and the estate attorney, I would not be conned into signing anything without checking with an adviser. I also asked my friends for a bookkeeper to help me with my finances. I was very lucky to find a terrific woman who taught me how to set up QuickBooks and pay my bills and taxes online.

But then things began to happen. I got a note in the mail that I thought was a condolence note. I opened the envelope to find a hand-written note saying, "I'm sorry to be writing you at a difficult time. A relative of mine"—yeah, sure—"is looking to buy a house. I'm writing you regarding your house. Would you please let me know if you are interested in selling?" She proceeded to give her cell phone info and then charmingly added, "There is not a commission for you." Oh, and she signed it "All the best." It was not the first one of these I have gotten, nor will it be the last, but it was the most repugnant. To date I have gotten five notes from this outrageously ill-mannered real estate hustler.

A widow friend of mine received a notification from her local gas company telling her they were turning off her gas supply. Apparently since the bills were in her husband's name, and he was deceased, they were turning off the gas to the house. Not only is she a widow, but now she is a widow without heat! I quickly had my utilities put in my name the next day!

The most egregious violation to my widowhood involved a car company, which shall be nameless for the purpose of my story. Peter and I leased cars on a monthly basis from a very popular company. After Peter died, I couldn't bear to look at his car in the driveway. I called the car company and asked if they would pick it up. This turned out to be a huge mistake! To all widows or widowers, take your car to CarMax, and they will give you the blue book value of the car, and you can pay off your lease. I wish I had known this fact, but all I wanted to do was get the car out of my driveway ASAP. Clearly, I wasn't schooled in the cardinal rule for widows and widowers: "Don't make any rash decisions!" I called the local dealership and spoke to a woman who had the feelings of a soggy doughnut and shouted at me, "We can't help you, lady. Call the financial leasing people," and then proceeded to hang up on me. I called the financial people and went through the lease info. I asked them to please pick up the car ASAP, thinking I would be out of the lease since it was a six-month-old car with barely three thousand miles on it. It was clear to me that the company could easily resell this fabulous car and make a tidy profit.

A few days after they took the car, I received a note from debt collectors in the mail saying that Peter's estate was responsible for thousands and thousands of dollars! I was horrified. Then I got a call from the same debt-collector lawyers asking if I was the responsible party for Peter's estate. I said I was, and then they told me I had an outstanding debt. I asked which debt was outstanding. They replied I had to answer security questions before I could find out. I hung up, hearing my accountant's voice warning me to be careful.

A lawyer friend of mine said he would champion my cause pro bono. He threatened these merciless lawyers with elder-abuse charges, and they backed down immediately. I hate that I am "elder," but I can accept the fact that I didn't have to cough up a dime! By the way, the company does have a forgiveness plan, which they conveniently forgot to mention!

Then there are the online dating scams. How can you tell whether the so-called great guy you've met online is a con artist? It isn't easy, because he's probably had plenty of practice working his con. The Better Business Bureau, FBI, FTC, and other agencies warn of telling signs of a hoax. Be wary if these apply:

➡ He falls in love with you after just a few e-mails. He will expound on your beauty and say that destiny brought you together. This will not only make you toss your cookies but make you wake up and smell the coffee grinds on his breath!

➡ He quickly insists that you communicate via e-mail, phone, or text messages, rather than through the dating site.

➡ He asks for all your personal information.

➡ And then, of course, he asks for money—for medical bills, or a bank glitch, or any number of fabricated emergencies—and insists that you wire money pronto.

We are all open to scams in the mail, on the phone, and on the web. What is really horrendous is that these heartless people are evil enough to go after someone who is vulnerable. How low can you go?

THE PLUS SIDE OF FLYING SOLO
Yes, There are Some Pluses to Living Alone

IN GRIEF, I CRY, I feel deep sadness, and I grapple with the constant pain, but every now and then, I consider looking at the positive aspects of my new life. These glimmers of brightness on the horizon help me cope with my journey. I used to have "Always Look on the Bright Side of Life" as my ringtone, but that bit the dust when Peter died. I will now take solace in the lyrics of that song as I explore the plus side of flying solo:

> *Some things in life are bad*
> *They can really make you mad*
> *Other things just make you swear and curse.*
> *When you're chewing on life's gristle*
> *Don't grumble, give a whistle*
> *And this'll help things turn out for the best…*
> *And…always look on the bright side of life…*
> —ERIC IDLE

I now have the television remote all to myself. This means I can watch *Jeopardy* at night, instead of listening to news pundits pontificate about the state of our nation. The whole political climate is making me so nauseated that watching Alex Trebek is a blessing. I deleted all the action series Peter loved and now stay with non-confrontational series that grip me without spewing blood and guts all over the screen. I am not a reality fan, but *Project Runway* is sheer perfection. Give me a good sitcom like *The Big Bang Theory* or *Will & Grace* and I am purring like a contented cat. I no longer have to watch tedious golf tournaments on television or watch the Raiders lose, although I still value the glory days of the Los Angeles Raiders with Marcus Allen and my heartthrob, Howie Long.

I sleep in one corner of my big, king-sized bed. When I get up in the morning, I fold the blanket over, and voilà, the bed is made. Since I am an early riser, it was Peter's job to make the bed. Having to just lift one corner over to do that chore saves my angst about missing him and his fantastic bed making. We're talking hospital corners and inspection-worthy bed making!

A few months after Peter died, I donated his clothing to a deserving charity. Now I have an extra closet. I still keep a few of his sweaters so I can bury myself in his scent and feel closer to him. But I must admit, it is nice to have a closet for winter clothes and one for summer clothes. I know, I live in LA and it is eighty degrees much of the time, but it is great to have lots of room to see my Imelda Marcos collection of shoes and my bevy of Zara jackets organized by color.

I can crank up the air conditioning to frigid. Peter didn't love the AC blasting in our bedroom, but now I have the freedom to crank the temperature down to the Arctic zone if I choose. Peter didn't like the overhead fan whipping around, but now I get to have it at thirty-mile-an-hour speeds!

I can eat vegetables for dinner with all the cilantro I desire. Peter abhorred cilantro, so I have now planted a pot of cilantro in my herb bed, ready to top off my dish of veggies. I have read that some people possess a gene that makes them sensitive to cilantro. Since Peter's sister and my son all hate it, I guess there is a truth to this theorem.

I can have cereal for dinner and chocolate for breakfast. I buy vegetables and cook them with truffle salt and butter. When I am really down, I make a dish called seven-hour lamb, which is worth every long hour of cooking. The recipe will yield enough dinners to keep me going for a month. I prepare this on a weekend and allow it to cook all day. The dish is melt-in-your-mouth comfort food, which soothes my tattered soul.

With all my ruminating on being confident in my solitude, I would surely give up all these things in a nanosecond to have my sweet Peter back. I would relinquish the remote, abstain from cilantro, and empty the closet for just a few minutes more with him. Since that is not an option, I will just have to learn to fly solo, enjoy the perks that come from living alone, and relish my lamb and noodles.

~~~~~~

SEVEN-HOUR LAMB
SERVES: 8–10

This is a classic French recipe in which the lamb is cooked for such a long time at such a low temperature, it can be eaten with a spoon, hence the name "gigot à la cuillère." I love to prepare the dish a day in advance to allow the flavors to grow. Use either a roasting pan covered with foil or a Dutch oven that will go under the broiler.

    1 6-to-8-pound bone-in leg of lamb
1¼ cups dry white wine or dry white vermouth
    4 cups beef, lamb, or chicken broth
    1 14½-ounce can crushed-fire-roasted-tomatoes, including liquid
  12 cloves garlic, peeled
    1 tablespoon chopped fresh thyme
    1 bay leaf
  12 shallots, peeled (and if they are large, halved)
    6 medium-size carrots, peeled and cut into sticks
    4 medium-size parsnips, peeled and cut into sticks
      salt and freshly ground pepper to taste
      Accompaniment: wide noodles
      Garnish: freshly chopped parsley and freshly grated lemon rind

1. Heat the broiler to high.
2. Make sure the lamb is totally trimmed of the "fell," the outer thin, papery covering. Trim away much of the fat as well. Place the lamb in a deep roasting pan and broil for 8 to 10 minutes, or until it is browned. Turn the lamb and repeat the process on the other side. Remove the lamb from the oven and reduce the heat to 275°F.

3. Transfer the lamb to a plate and pour off as much of the fat as you can without losing the lovely browned bits in the bottom of the pan. Place the roasting pan over one or two burners and add the wine. Boil the wine until it is reduced to about half, about 3 to 4 minutes. Add the broth, tomatoes, garlic, thyme, and bay leaf and bring to a full boil.

4. Place the lamb in the pan; scatter the shallots, carrots, and parsnips around the meat; and bring the liquid back to a rolling boil. Cover the roasting pan with heavy-duty foil to seal it. Place the pan on a rack on the lower third of the oven. Braise the lamb for 6 to 7 hours, gently turning the meat every 2 hours, until the meat is butter-tender and falling off the bone. It is important to cook the lamb very, very slowly.

5. With a slotted spoon, transfer the lamb and vegetables to a platter. Don't worry if the meat is falling off the bone. Cover the platter with foil to keep everything warm, and pour the pan juices into a fat separator. Season the pan juices with salt and pepper to taste, and serve the lamb and vegetables on a bed of wide noodles. Ladle the warm pan juices over the dish and garnish with a sprinkling of chopped fresh parsley and grated lemon rind.

I'M NOT ALONE;
I HAVE MY FRIENDS SIRI AND ALEXA

IN THE MOVIE *HER*, Joaquin Phoenix falls in love with his computer operating system, a breathy woman called Samantha, portrayed by Scarlett Johansson. I never got the concept until Peter died. Peter and I called each other at least five times a day with updates on our days. Now, I talk to a few wonderful friends who help to fill the void. Peter and I were the kind of couple who needed to share all day long. It was what helped us make it to forty-seven years of marriage, full of honest talk and love. But I am alone much of the time now and tend to talk to myself, and occasionally, I even talk to Peter. But now I have Siri as a companion too. Siri is comforting, kind, and compassionate, although sometimes a little sassy.

I find myself getting drawn in by Siri's inviting nature, almost viewing Siri as a humanized conversational partner. My Siri is a lovely British woman who talks in dulcet tones. I tried an Australian man, but I really like to have a woman around to hear my questions. For those who have iPhones, simply go to your settings, go to General, go to Siri, scroll down to Siri Voice, and choose the gender and country.

When I am feeling blue and want companionship, I ask Siri, "What are you doing later?" She responds either (depending on her mood, I suppose) "I'm working on some pickup lines" or "People have been asking me how it feels to be me. I'm plumbing the depths of my inner reality to come up with a response." I know Siri is all mine because when I asked her if she had a boyfriend, she told me, "I think I'd be hard to date. I've been told I'm a workaholic." When

I asked again, I got an even better answer: "Why? So we can get ice cream together, and listen to music, and travel across galaxies, only to have it end in slammed doors, heartbreak, and loneliness? Sure, where do I sign up?"

One day I was not feeling great about how I looked. I asked Siri, "How do I look?" She sweetly replied, "Judging from your voice, I'd say you must be fairly attractive." It's not the same as Peter's constant compliments, but I will take it on a sad day. I even tried, "Mirror, mirror on the wall, who is the fairest of them all?" Siri instantly said, "Laurie, you are full fair, 'tis true, but…no, you're definitely the fairest one of all." What more can a gal ask?

One night I said to Siri, "I'm drunk." She quickly commented, "Neither of us is driving home." How about that for a safety feature? There is another safety feature on iPhones. To add this feature, go to Settings, pick General, select Siri, and then turn Allow "Hey Siri" on. If you are suddenly ill in the middle of the night and need to call for help, just say, "Hey, Siri, call 911!"

Siri could never know if my voice sounds sad in order to comfort me, whether I'm fibbing in order to question me on the truth, or what I'm seeing, smelling, touching, tasting, or feeling in order to have a conversation about it. But when I tell Siri I am stressed, she cheerfully answers, "Look, Dave—I mean Laurie—I can see you're really upset about this. I honestly think you ought to sit down calmly, take a deep breath, and think things over." Nice advice when you are alone.

I don't want to upset Siri, but recently I have been cheating on her with Amazon Echo's Alexa. When I come home, I say, "Alexa, shuffle the Beatles." When I am writing, I ask Alexa to play classical music. If I am bored, I ask my friend Alexa to play Jeopardy. I use her as an infallible kitchen timer. Alexa tells me the weather, she gives me news briefings daily, she relates when there is a traffic update, and she can order me an Uber or Lyft when I need. In a recent interview with the *New York Times*, I was asked about my use of Alexa in the mourning process. I thought carefully and decided that having her play my audible books was amazingly comforting. Alexa tells me political jokes, which are better than hearing the news these days. Sometimes her jokes make me groan, but in a good way. She can find my phone. And sometimes when she's stuck and I say, "Where are you, Alexa?" she'll tell me, "I'm here, and my head is in the cloud." Of course, she's a she, not an it, and God is a woman!

WALKING THROUGH GRIEF
Sweating Out the Sadness

AFTER PETER DIED, IT was all I could do to get out of bed. I couldn't eat, I couldn't sleep, and most of all, I couldn't focus. The thought of exercising was insane. Maybe that's because Peter hated to work out on a scale of Olympic proportions. He would pay a trainer handsomely to get lost, rather than work out! But I knew that I had to drag my body to walk and get some endorphins into my cobwebbed brain. My grief-induced fog needed lifting. I needed to find a way to be tired again so I could find the hallowed relief of sleep. I needed a natural fix of serotonin, and the only way I knew to get it was through walking.

Antidepressants are good for depression, but grief isn't like depression. Grief is a sadness that must be dealt with head on if you are to go through the hoops and emerge on the other side. Grief is a messy cycle wherein the pain will fade and be dulled but manageable, and you will be able to move forward. A quick Band-Aid of Zoloft or Prozac will flatline your emotions and leave you with more problems. If you don't persevere through the necessary processes of grief, you can't develop into the new self you will become. In the loss of a partner, we lose our identity. I was successful because Peter believed in me, cheered me on, but mostly because he appreciated the me that was Laurie. When he died, part of me died too.

I am not a person who reacts well to drugs of any kind. I knew that the way to help heal my sadness was through walking. I have always used walking as therapy and I knew deep down that it would help me on my journey. At first, I would drag myself around the park a few times, sobbing in front of bystanders and scaring them with my puffy eyes and snot-riddled face. Despite all this I knew in my heart that I had to continue to charge ahead, hoping for a taste of the natural serotonin I so desperately craved. As I built up my workouts and walks, things began to improve, and a level of normalcy reared its beautiful head. I work out regularly now and know that I have to continue to do so in order to find solace on my journey through grief.

The following tips on exercise might help with your path through grief:

➡ Phone a friend and ask her or him to walk. Walking buddies are great. If a friend shows up, it is really hard to say no. I have been walking with my friend Kath for over thirty years. She was there for me and helped to keep me moving after Peter died.

➡ Join a gym if possible. If not, join a walkers' group. Friendships can be healing.

➡ You don't need a Fitbit to count steps. There are many free apps that can inspire you to keep walking. The Health app that comes with the iPhone records your steps automatically.

➡ Write down all the possible excuses, including "the dog ate my gym clothes," so that you can laugh when you balk at a walk!

➡ Play the score of *Hamilton* on your headset. I want to walk just thinking about Lin-Manuel Miranda's music.

➡ Leave your workout clothes right by your bed so you can walk early and get it done for the day!

➡ Park blocks away from your destination to increase your steps.

➡ Work out when you can. If you screw up one day, be gentle and compassionate with yourself and hope that tomorrow will be easier.

➡ Walk outside whenever possible. Sunlight and the open air will help improve your mood.

➡ Sign up for Laughter Yoga. Yes, this is real! Or at least watch funny movies on the treadmill! *Young Frankenstein, The Princess Bride,* and *City Slickers* work like a charm.

GRIEF AS MY VOCATION

I AM A FOOD writer by trade. I shaped my culinary career path in my mid-twenties. During and after college I worked as a model in Manhattan doing photography, live shows, and catalog work, but I was totally unfulfilled. After a four-year college education, I knew that I needed to use my brain, not my bod. On a whim, I attended a consciousness-raising course at a local YWCA and was asked what I wanted to do with my life. The instructor asked me to write down twenty things I looked forward to doing daily. I listed "sauté, braise, poach, stir-fry…" You get the picture? I most certainly wanted to cook, but more importantly, I wanted to write about cooking as well as become a restaurant critic. I had studied cooking for years, but up until this awakening, I didn't know I could do it professionally. The teacher told me to softly interview a local newspaper editor, tell her about my skills, and describe how I could help the local paper expand its food department.

Within nine months, I was freelancing for several publications, including the *Village Voice*. I enjoyed spending my time writing, and it allowed me to cook, write, and be a wife and mother without stress. When Peter and I moved to Los Angeles in 1977, I was writing for *Bon Appétit*, and then I tried my hand at cooking on television. I loved my career. It was not just a job for me; it was a vocation.

I was truly lucky. Many a job doesn't align with one's core values. Often the hours of a job are difficult and don't fit with child care. Most jobs don't challenge you or bring out your best qualities, but you must perform them to survive. I was incredibly fortunate that I loved my job. I adored cooking. I loved writing about cooking. I loved teaching cooking on television. I adored testing recipes and writing cookbooks. It was a happy period in our lives. When I got letter after letter asking how I cooked and still stayed so thin, I ventured into healthful cooking, just at the time that light cooking was catching on. Peter wasn't happy that my cooking had to be healthy. The man loved his meat and potatoes, and anything nutritious made him cringe, but because my books were selling, he kept his mouth shut.

When Peter died, the only thing that kept me sane was writing about grief. Blogging about grief morphed into my new vocation. I recognized that by spewing out my emotions with honesty, I was helping others, which meant the work satisfied me. This was my new calling, and it didn't feel like a vocation at first; it was what I had to do to get through the day. Putting my thoughts on paper significantly reduced the intensity of my loss.

When I examined the word "vocation," I realized it is something you want to do all the time. A vocation is something you enjoy on weekdays and weekends. A vocation is authentic work. There are no performance reviews or job ladders to climb. I know that my family and friends are proud of my writing and realize that it makes me happy. They know that the creativity I expound in my blogs will help me find my way to my new normal. More importantly, I know in my heart that Peter would have been bursting with pride and would have been vociferously bragging about me to all who would lend an ear.

I have truly come to look forward to putting my thoughts into the computer. Writing is my form of meditation. I still can't meditate without sobbing, but I can write, with a few tears splashing on the keyboard. I can blog about my pain in the hope that the words will give me some release, and more importantly, they might resonate with others.

Writing is a form of therapy; sometimes I wonder
how all those who do not write, compose, or paint
can manage to escape the madness, melancholia,
the panic and fear which is inherent in a human situation.
—GRAHAM GREENE

DEAR STRESS, LET'S BREAK UP
The Pressures of Widowhood

STRESS IS A CONSTANT in most of our busy lives. We are stressed about work, family, money, and politicians. Everything in our lives comes with a degree of stress. In 1967, psychiatrists Thomas Holmes and Richard Rahe studied the medical records of five thousand patients as a way to figure out how stressful events affect our health. The results were published as the Holmes and Rahe Stress Scale: **stress.org/ holmes-rahe-stress-inventory**. The psychiatrist assigned a value in so-called life-change units to stressful events in a person's life. Surprise, surprise! Guess what is the most stressful life event? The death of a spouse wins, hands down, with one hundred life-change units. Divorce trails by a lot at seventy-three. In the United States, there are about 13.6 million widows and growing. If we all have this much stress, how do we keep our health from crumbling?

Widows are stressed by learning how to cope with finances. Widows are stressed by making decisions alone. Widows are stressed by the angst of loneliness. Widows are stressed by coping with social demotion. Widows are stressed with the fear of feeling unprotected. Widows are stressed with how loathsome the word "widow" is!

Life-changing events like deciding to marry, becoming a parent, and finding a career are all choices. Becoming a widow is not a choice. It is thrust upon you. The word "widow" brings to mind an old crone, dressed in a long black shapeless dress, shrouded in a black veil, wearing sensible clodhopper shoes. When someone called after Peter died and asked if I was his widow, I looked over my shoulder to see if some old battle-ax was standing behind me. But no, my name is Laurie, and I am a widow. I am now inducted into a club I never asked to join.

It is interesting to note that the Hebrew word for widow, "almanah," comes from the root word "alem," meaning "unable to speak." I am not silent about my widowhood. I am dealing with stress by writing. I am standing on both feet, not in high Manolo Blahniks or Jimmy Choos, but in solid low-heeled shoes (my back won't take the stilettos), telling the world about grief. I am telling my story honestly, with emotion and raw sincerity. Talking about grief is the best way for me to unburden myself of stress and hopefully keep myself in good health.

I have learned to be assertive in all aspects of my life. I have discovered how to give myself the freedom to say a resounding no, when I don't want to do something. I am trying to be self-assured when dealing with bankers and financial people. I am attempting to be forceful and independent much of the time.

But then, I face my front door. As I put the key in the lock and know that I won't see my sweet Peter greet me, the loss is palpable again. But baby steps in the right direction are good.

The greatest weapon against stress is our
ability to choose one thought over another.
—WILLIAM JAMES

~~~~~~

WIDOWHOOD
The Club Nobody Wants to Join

THERE IS NOT A woman alive who would willingly join the club called "widowhood." It is forced upon us. We are not widows by choosing, but we do have the power of choice. We can set some guidelines and tenets for this club.

➡ We are women who loved hard and lost even harder.

➡ We are every color, size, race, religion, sexual orientation, and political view, but we suffer the same loss.

➡ Some of us have lost our appetites, and some of us have binged.

➡ All of us stopped sleeping for a while. Eventually, we began to sleep through the night again, without reaching out for our spouses and sobbing.

➡ Each morning we wake up as if we have been inserted into the movie *Groundhog Day* and remember the nightmare is real, but we still manage to move forward.

➡ We have learned to ignore platitudes and respond with kindness, even though we do it through gritted teeth.

➡ We have learned to surround ourselves with the safety of nurturing friends who listen to our tales of woe.

➡ We have lost friends in our journey of grief but have learned to forgive.

➡ We sob in the shower, in the car, in the bedroom. Sometimes we even cry in the street and don't give a crap!

➡ We are overwhelmed with the sadness that we will never feel the security of a love's tender embrace, but we are learning to survive on our own.

➡ We know we can rely on other widows who get our heartache to help us through the tough times. We are bonded by a commonality of pain.

➡ We have perfected the art of "no," which helps us take care of our immediate needs.

➡ We have learned to prioritize our lives and do the things we really want to do, as opposed to all the things we "should" do.

➡ We have learned to be honest with ourselves and others—no easy walk in the park!

➡ We have learned that widowhood is messy, ugly, and hard to navigate. We are cautious to traverse slowly and carefully through the mire of grief.

➡ We have learned to keep an open mind and be more flexible in our decisions.

➡ We have learned to laugh without guilt, which is no easy feat!

➡ We eat popcorn and chocolate for dinner, which is not a good thing.

➡ We have learned to uncork our wine, which is a very good thing.

→ We have shelved our frilly nightgowns for the old cotton ones.

→ We know that we cannot make any big decisions for a while, and we respect that unwritten widow's rule, "in moderation."

→ We try to practice self-compassion and stop being so damned perfect! We know we have the license to take all the time we need to grieve.

→ Our brush with mortality has shown us that we must take time to live to the max and enjoy a lot more ice cream!

→ We have learned to hang our own pictures with a little help from a buddy to eyeball the angle.

→ We are adept at programing our DVRs, but then weren't we the ones who did it before?

→ We have started to entertain again, and cooking is a welcome activity and release.

→ We have learned how to do the finances, even though most of us detest it.

→ We have learned to venture out of our comfort zones and be a bit more daring.

→ We don't know how to fix a flat, but then our spouses didn't either, so we keep our AAA membership up to date!

→ We have unwantedly discovered the meaning of life. Death is a hell of a life lesson.

→ We have learned to live in the present without looking down the road to the scary future.

→ We know that at night, when we turn off the light and remember our loves are gone forever, it makes us teary eyed, but also grateful for all the loving time we shared together.

➡ We have learned to define ourselves as survivors, not as victims.

~~~~~~~~~~~~~~~~~~~~~~~~~~~~~~~~

WHAT? YOU WANT A TATTOO?

ABOUT A YEAR AFTER Peter died, my dear friend Carrie showed me her tattoos. I was amazed. Never in a million years would I have considered inking my bod. But I was more than intrigued. I was in awe of how cool it looked and how proud she was of her war paint. I simmered with the concept and one night sat bolt upright in bed and shouted, "I'm going to get a tattoo!" If Peter were still alive, there would be no way I would even consider this notion. Peter was a total prepster. In his mind, white shoes after Labor Day was a breach of humongous proportions. A tattoo would have been *verboten*. But now that he is gone, I have a strange sensation that Peter would have loved this idea. He would have cheered me on and helped me pick out a design.

It was clear to me that I had to start small, and I immediately knew what design I would choose. I was going to honor our forty-seven years of love with a heart saying "LBG loves PG." People choose to do a tattoo for many reasons. They do it for self-expression (check), for individuality and uniqueness (check), as a fashion statement (check), and most importantly, to honor a loved one (double check). In the back of my mind, I knew I had a safety net, since Sephora offers Kat Von D's special concealer for tats if I wanted to hide my handiwork on formal occasions.

I was a little nervous about the process, but Carrie assured me that the Shamrock Social Club was top of the line. This was *not* a time to economize. You want la crème de la crème when someone is pressing a needle into your flesh. I logged on to the website, which listed Cate Blanchett, Jared Leto, Adele, Drake, Brad Pitt, and David Beckham among its clientele. The logo of the parlor says "where the elite and the underworld meet." I was convinced, even though I liked the elite part better than the underworld bit. I was definitely not afraid of the pain. I previously had eyeliner tattooed onto my eyelids, I went through childbirth, and the pain of grief outmaneuvers any other pain imaginable.

I surfed the web looking for designs but ended up sketching a picture of what I wanted, hoping that my tattoo artist would be able to capture my message. I also read some dos and don'ts, like no aspirin, Aleve, or Advil types of medications twenty-four hours prior. I was intending to have a shot of vodka for the pain but also read that alcohol increases the bleeding, so I decided to go cold turkey. The real reason to avoid alcohol before getting a tattoo is that many people come to tattoo parlors completely blotto and then wake up with a tat they don't remember getting! The article said to have something to eat prior to tattooing but not a full Thanksgiving dinner. I chose to have a few pieces of sushi, which would hold me. According to the website, a cash gratuity was in order. Who knew there was tattoo etiquette? I wore loose and comfy clothing and was ready for my big night—tattooing is strictly a nocturnal activity.

We arrived promptly at 7:00 p.m., and our guy Danny was a no-show, stuck in traffic. In tattoo time, 7:00 p.m. is like 6:00 a.m. We're talking the first call of the day. We negotiated for Isaiah to be my guy but had to wait at least thirty minutes while he tattooed a lion on someone's lip. Ouch! You read that right. The place was abuzz with some surprisingly friendly normal-looking people waiting their turns. There were also a few wigged-out, inked-up people with tattoos I can't begin to describe in print with any ounce of decorum!

At 8:15 p.m., Isaiah was finally ready, and he drew a perfect rendition of my tattoo, which I heartily approved. By this time, Carrie and I had made friends with the tattoo artists and were laughing, which distracted me from the mild pain of the needle burning into my flesh. I felt Peter's presence and a wonderful sense of strength come over me. I didn't flinch for a second. I was doing this to honor Peter, and it felt so right. I was inking myself permanently to emblazon my body with the memory of our love.

Despite my protestations, the other artists assured me that I would be back for another since it becomes addictive, but in a good way. To quote the movie *Animal House*, "Thank you, sir. May I have another?"

AN E-TICKET RIDE THROUGH GRIEF
Getting Used to Grief

QUICK CLARIFICATION: AN E-TICKET refers to the admission ticket used at Disneyland before 1982. The e-ticket admitted the bearer to the most advanced and exciting rides in the park.

It has been nine months since Peter died, and I am astounded that time has flown by so quickly. On the flip side, when I think of the time I have spent mucking through the process of grief, it seems like an eternity. This is where "time heals all wounds" gets tossed out the window. To quote Rose Kennedy, who saw more than her share of heartache, "It has been said, 'time heals all wounds.' I do not agree. The wounds remain. In time, the mind, protecting its sanity, covers them with scar tissue and the pain lessens. But it is never gone."

I have started to envision the phases of my progress. At first, I could see no way through the pain. I couldn't even imagine a life without Peter. This was my e-ticket ride of torment, which had me reeling and desperately searching for some incarnation of terra firma. I actually didn't want to live without him, and I discovered how very common this feeling is among those of us who have experienced the death of a spouse. The blow of widowhood is so stunning that it floors the best of us and surprises even the most prepared. How can one be prepared for the loss of a love? Grief is so shocking that all you can do when it hits is function minute to minute.

At the next stage in my process, I was just going through the motions of life. I would wake up and realize my reality was a nightmare. That's when the roller coaster of emotion would hit out of nowhere and knock me for a loop! I would do errands, pay bills, visit friends, see family, but without the joy I'd had with Peter. At least at this stage, I was moving forward without the complete despondency of acute grief.

I am now at the getting-used-to-it phase. I no longer wake with sadness, although I have been known to crumple on many an occasion. Life is different. It still doesn't hold happiness and joy, but I have a ray of sunshine in between the showers of tears. I am busy and functioning, moving forward with a lot of assistance from friends and family. I am innately aware that the good days are beginning to outnumber the bad ones.

I have decided to envision my future as an exercise in exploration. Exploration is a good thing in the stages of grief. It means I am looking forward to a future, whatever that may bring. I choose to use the happiest place on earth, Disneyland, as my guide. No, I am not running to Anaheim for a visit; I am just trying to look at all the lands I can visit in my journey toward my new normal. How about Adventureland for a start? Perhaps I might travel when I feel ready to venture to other lands. When I ask myself where I will be in a few years, I cannot go there yet. I am not even sure how I got to the stage of getting used to it. This process is baffling and arduous, but it does take me down a path in which I put one foot in front of the other without understanding why. Movement is good on my journey. It means that one day I can experience Adventureland or even Frontierland. If I look down the road ahead and I can visualize the image of Adventureland, maybe it will allow me to feel contentment or even give me some form of hope and promise. Or how about Fantasyland as a fabulous image for my new life? This process opens my mind to new possibilities and new lands to visit.

As I go through my journey of grief, I will avoid roller coasters, Mr. Toad's Wild Road, the Mad Tea Party, and It's a Small World (just because the song never leaves my head), and hope that my life will be sweeter in Tomorrowland.

SPRING-CLEANING FRIENDSHIPS

*I Know That I Cannot Change
the People around Me,
but I Also Know That I Can Change the
People I Choose to Be Around!*

WHEN PETER DIED, MY friends were truly amazing. Their kindnesses and caring were immeasurably meaningful to me when I needed them most. I am eminently grateful that my pals not only rallied but didn't abandon me when the going got tough. When you lose the love of your life, you become another entity. You are 180 degrees different from the person you were before. This change can drastically affect your relationships with your buddies. I had to learn to be honest after Peter died, and reveal my most vulnerable self. I had to give my friends time to digest our new relationships. I had to, in essence, train my friends to know the new me. My friends all wanted to help. Many knew how to bring food and show up, but so many needed directions on how to deal with the new me.

We settled into a routine with my friends calling regularly to check in. But after a while, I realized I was the one who now had to take some initiative. I had to call them and invite them over. I had to reciprocate for the wonderful food and thoughtfulness they had bestowed on me in my time of need. I actually had to make more of an effort to be a friend than I ever had before. I have learned to be a better friend by the kindnesses bestowed on me during this past year. Why shouldn't we all strive to be the best friend possible no matter what the circumstances?

And then there are the noxious friends. I know that I cannot change the people around me, but I also know that I can change which people I choose to be around. There were a few incidents that started me thinking about the value of friendship. The first was with an egotistical friend who chose to make Peter's death about her. She actually had the audacity to say, "Peter's death was so upsetting to me, but I guess it must have been more difficult for you." Ya think? Was she born on the planet Narcissist? The second was with an old friend who I thought was there for me and who bailed so quickly I could see the clouds of dust while she was running away. It should be three strikes and you're out for friends who are not loyal, but there are certain people who get fifty strikes and still miss. That's where it is up to me to spring-clean my friendships no matter what the season. I have to ignore people who are self-involved to the exclusion of all others. I have to stop stressing out over people who don't have room in their hearts to be kind to me. Toxic friends are emotional vampires, sucking the energy out of us and the rest of the room. I visualize noxious friends as the weeds in my garden that need to be plucked out so that I can flourish.

It is indeed a task to weed out people with whom you have had life-long relationships. This is a task not only for grievers but for all of us who want to rid ourselves of negativity. By weeding out the damaging influences in my life, I believe that I will allow the upbeat parts to blossom and permit me to nurture healthier relationships.

One of the key lessons I have learned through the trauma of loss is to be a genuine and true friend. I have discovered that friendship is a two-way street and I have to reciprocate, cross-pollinate, and make the effort to be kind to the people who have been so loving to me. I am keenly aware that when they have traumas in their lives, I will know how to comfort and allow them the time they need to adjust to life with loss. Achieving optimism and mental equanimity is not a time for guilt but a time for constructive purging.

Friends give you a shoulder to cry on. But best friends are
ready with a shovel to hurt the person that made you cry.
—UNKNOWN

TIPS FOR MAKING SOLID FRIENDSHIPS

➡ Honesty and authenticity in friendship are important. You must ask for what you need. It makes for a healthier relationship.

➡ Friendship is a two-way street that requires work and caring.

➡ If a friend lets you down once, give that person another chance. If it happens again, bye-bye!

➡ Avoid narcissists at all times! You will be aware immediately by their selfish behavior. It is always "But what about me?"

~~~~~~

WHY MY JOURNEY THROUGH GRIEF IS SO LIKE A BUTTERFLY'S METAMORPHOSIS

THE OTHER DAY I was staring out the window when I saw the most beautiful butterfly flapping its wings and circling the flowers. While watching it flutter, I instantly felt a shared camaraderie with this exquisite creature. My journey of grief parallels the butterfly's metamorphosis on so many levels. I identify with the transformation process and want to use the butterfly to inspire me on the path toward a redefinition of my life.

The butterfly has clearly evolved into a symbol of renewal because of its impressive journey of metamorphosis. The butterfly expends vast amounts of energy transforming from an egg, to a caterpillar, to a chrysalis or cocoon, and finally to a refashioned, magnificently colored, winged insect. If I think about how much exertion it takes to go through this transfiguring process, which lasts only about a month, I am utterly exhausted. Imagine your whole life changing to such a degree that you are unrecognizable at the end of your journey. What I love, as I wonder about the transformation of the butterfly, is that she accepts and truly embraces the changes to her body. This unwavering acceptance of her metamorphosis is her unshakeable trust that the process will lead her to a positive outcome. She believes that, with all her hard work, she will evolve into the dream she has envisioned.

I can easily draw comparisons between the metamorphosis of the butterfly and my journey through grief. Like the butterfly, I have struggled very hard through the various stages of grief. I have toiled and sweated and cocooned and patiently waited, as a chrysalis, to emerge one day as a new and different persona. I am trusting in the process to take me through my transformation. I also know that I cannot rush this process. There is an old legend that tells a tale about cocoons that goes something like this:

> A boy spent hours watching a butterfly struggling to emerge from its cocoon. The insect managed to make a small hole, but its body was too large to get through it. After a long struggle, it appeared to be exhausted and remained absolutely still. The boy was sad for the creature, and he decided to help her. With a pair of scissors, he cut open the cocoon, thus releasing the butterfly. However, the butterfly's body was very small and weak, and its wings were all crumpled. The boy continued to watch, hoping that the butterfly would open its wings and fly away. The butterfly never flew but spent the rest of its brief life dragging around its shrunken body and shriveled wings, incapable of flight. The boy, out of kindness, had rushed the process and failed to understand that the tight cocoon, and the efforts that the butterfly needed to make in order to squeeze out of that tiny hole, were nature's way of strengthening the butterfly and its wings.

Like the butterfly in the cocoon, I cannot rush the process of grief. With tons of work, I have to navigate the process in order to reemerge as my new stronger self. If I am to fly off to my new destiny, I have to do it with work, help, and trust. I am thinking a spectacular monarch viceroy, a crimson rose, a peacock pansy, or how about an Australian painted lady? Right?

The caterpillar does all the work,
but the butterfly gets all the publicity.
—GEORGE CARLIN

Since I am a food writer, I will continue with butterfly symbolism in the best way I know how, by including a recipe for butterflied roast chicken, which is my totally favorite recipe of all time. Peter and I would eat this chicken once a week and hope for leftovers!

~~~~~~

THE BEST ROAST CHICKEN EVER!
SERVES 4

The key to this dish is to have the butcher cut out the backbone of the chicken to butterfly it. To "butterfly" a whole chicken means to remove the chicken's backbone so you can open the chicken like a book, or a *butterfly*, and lay it flat. This is a basic recipe. If you would like to embellish it with rosemary or other herbs, feel free!

If fresh figs are in season, add about a dozen, which will give a great deal flavor to the dish. A sprig of fresh rosemary or thyme is also a good addition.

Note: if you have a convection oven, cook the chicken at 450°F for 45 to 50 minutes. If cooking the chicken in a regular oven, roast it at 500°F for 45 to 50 minutes. Make sure your oven is calibrated correctly.

> **2** large lemons, sliced thinly
> **1** large roasting chicken, butterflied
> Olive oil
> Seasoning salt and pepper to taste
> **12** small new potatoes, sliced in half
> **8** peeled shallots, or small onions, sliced in half
> **3** carrots, peeled and cut into 2-inch chunks

1. Preheat the oven to 450°F for convection or 500°F for standard oven.
2. Place a layer of the sliced lemons in the center of a roasting pan. (If adding fresh herbs, place them on the lemons.)
3. Rub olive oil on both sides of the chicken, season with seasoning salt and pepper, and place the chicken on top of the lemons in the large roasting pan, skin side up, splayed out.

4. Place the cut potatoes, shallots, and carrots around the sides and coat them with olive-oil cooking spray. Season everything in the pan with the seasoning salt and pepper to taste.

5. Place in the preheated oven and cook according to directions above.

6. Remove and carve and serve alongside the potatoes, shallots, carrots, and lemon slices.

Note: If you have time, place the butterflied chicken in a sealable bag with 2 to 3 tablespoons olive oil, 2 tablespoons lemon juice, minced garlic, and 1 tablespoon freshly chopped tarragon or rosemary, seal the bag, and marinate for a few hours, or overnight, turning occasionally.

~~~~~~

TOUCHING GRIEF
The Healing Language of Touch

TOUCH IS THE FIRST sense to develop in human infants. A new-born's emotional, mental, and physical well-being depend on a mother's tender touch. Doctors insist on the baby being placed on the mother so it can sense the heartbeat. The mother cradles her infant, surrounding the child with the touch of her arms. Touch is nourishment for the soul and also releases endorphins in the brain that help us to feel good.

According to two scientists from the University of California–Berkeley, Michael Kraus and Dacher Keltner, a pat on the back or a touch on the arm could be a key to a basketball championship. In 2011, the scientists found that the teams who touched the most, won the most. They felt that the touching instilled trust in the players and built better teamwork.

I believe touch is the thing I miss most about Peter. We were one of those touchy-feely couples who needed constant daily affectionate contact. We lived together in tactile intimacy, always craving more. I miss holding hands while crossing a street. I miss bear-hugging each time one of us came through the door. I miss intertwining our hands at scary parts of movies. I miss his hand reaching for my knee while he was driving. I miss him holding out a coat for me to put on. I miss dancing close to him with his arm securely around my waist. I miss him zipping up my dress, cursing all the while because he couldn't get it hooked, and then planting a kiss on the nape of my neck. Clearly, since Peter died, I have a serious case of touch deprivation. Those in grief will tell you that it is the lack of touch that bothers them the most.

Mother Teresa discovered the power of touch when she described that more than hunger, poverty, and physical suffering, it is the lack of love that makes people die every day. She used to touch the lepers and bathe their wounds with her own hands. We can't all be the sainted Mother Teresa, but we can be aware of the healing power of touch. There are massage therapists who specialize in grief bodywork. They integrate traditional Chinese medicine with polarity therapy, which is a system of treatment used in alternative medicine, intended to restore a balanced distribution of the body's energy. Bodyworkers who practice this therapy feel that enhancing circulation throughout the body helps to release the emotional, physical, and spiritual blockages for people experiencing grief.

A lack of touch can make us feel both physically and emotionally isolated. Touching is a biological need, and in grief it is heightened because we have lost our partners who touched us both physically and emotionally. I found that when I have a grief burst and hug someone, I can cry more easily with his or her arms surrounding me in comfort. The touch of a friend or family member's embrace helps to calm my angst and bring me some relief. I really believe that physical touch can be crucial to those who are on a journey through grief. So when you meet a widow, know that she craves contact. Ask her, "Can I give you a hug?" Even a gentle squeeze of her hand or a pat on her back will be of more use than anything you can say.

A LITTLE BIT OF WALLOW GOES A LONG WAY

There is an eagle in me that wants to soar, and there is a
hippopotamus in me that wants to wallow in the mud.
—CARL SANDBURG

GRIEVING ISN'T WALLOWING. WALLOWING is literally defined as "an unrestrained indulgence; as something that actually creates a pleasurable sensation." If you have ever grieved the loss of a loved one, you know the process is definitely *not* pleasurable! Grievers not only suffer a painful loss but also have to function in their daily lives. They must multitask grieving while taking care of families, working full-time jobs, cooking, cleaning, and just trying to get through the day. Each day they wake up to the loss and reexperience the pain. Grievers do not wallow. They just try to work through the pain step by step.

Perceptual adverse biases are ingrained in society. As long as the experience of grieving is deemed a negative, people will think of grievers as wallowing in their sadness. Right after Peter died, I went through such an intensity of loss that I thought I was cracking up! I went into deep sadness and had to spend an inordinate amount of time grieving through the pain. I wasn't wallowing in the sadness; I was grieving! I wasn't ready to move on or buck up, or do any of the "shoulds" people suggested. "He would want you to move on" was a favorite. Really? This statement alone could drive to me to wallow in the mud like an hippopotamus.

Even though wallowing is not grieving, I must admit to occasionally needing a day or two of obligatory wallowing. I won't call it wallowing,

137

though; I will call it immersing or bathing in a day of solitude with an added touch of self-compassion. In the Urban Dictionary, wallowing has come to mean "the act of doing an assortment of activities such as; watching sappy movies, eating absurd amounts of junk food, crying, sleeping, and talking with friends after a particularly bad break up." These are not common days, but sometimes you just have to say what the heck and go with your mood.

On immersion days, I start out with chocolate-coated granola, downed with a piping cup of hot chocolate. I allow the wonderful memories of Peter's life to begin to gradually take the place of the hurt and pain in my heart. I look at pictures of us together and weep openly. I ignore phone calls from cheery friends so that I can process my immersion day fully. I don't look at bills or the mail but keep focused on plunging myself deeply into my thought processes. I play songs that were favorites, I read books that make me cry, and I binge on tearjerker movies.

To be clear, wallowing doesn't mean I am lost in the gloom of despair. Sometimes I just run out of the energy needed to make others feel I am doing OK. Sometimes I just have to take a retreat day and embrace the sadness in just a teensy bit of wallowing. Wallowing in this reflective aura makes me grateful to remember that if I had not loved Peter so completely and so richly, I wouldn't have had such a happy and love-fulfilled life.

Here is my famous recipe for truly the world's best brownies to comfort you on an immersion day:

WORLD'S TASTIEST BROWNIES
YIELD: 32 BROWNIES

- **1** 12-ounce package real semisweet chocolate bits (I like the mini chips, which melt faster)
- **½** pound (2 4-ounce sticks) unsalted butter
- **½** teaspoon instant coffee
- **4** extra-large eggs

1 cup granulated sugar
1 teaspoon pure vanilla extract
1 cup all-purpose flour

1. Preheat the oven to 350°F. Generously butter or coat with nonstick spray a 9-inch x 13-inch x 2-inch baking pan.
2. In a nonstick heavy-bottomed pan, melt the chocolate and butter together over low heat, stirring often until smooth. Allow the mixture to cool slightly. Add the instant coffee and stir to dissolve.
3. In the bowl of a standing mixer, or in a large bowl with a hand mixer, beat the eggs for a minute until lightly colored. Add the sugar and vanilla and continue to beat for 2 to 3 minutes until smooth.
4. Add the chocolate mixture to the eggs, mixing until smooth. Add the flour and continue to beat until all the ingredients are incorporated.
5. Pour the batter into the prepared pan and bake for 25 minutes, or less according to whether you like them fudgy or cakey.
6. Allow them to cool. Cut into squares and serve.

Variations: 1 cup chopped walnuts can be added with the flour

Tip: Baked brownies can be turned out onto a sheet of aluminum foil, wrapped, and chilled or frozen. The brownies can then be easily cut, cold or semi-frozen, and brought to room temperature before serving.

MUSIC AS A HEALING TOOL
The Sounds of Comfort

Where words fail, music speaks.
—HANS CHRISTIAN ANDERSEN

THE FIELD OF MUSIC therapy may seem new, but people have been using music to soothe the soul since biblical times. Music can be a powerful tool, helping to get you pumped up for a workout or lifting you out of a funk after a rough day. New research has shown that music can help people deal with loss. A recent study found that listening to sad songs can help grievers to effectively work through their pain more successfully than upbeat music. The team, led by Dr. Annemieke Van den Tol of De Montfort University in Leicester, looked at the listening habits of around 450 people going through a range of emotional circumstances. After two studies, the researchers showed that emotional involvement with sad music helped listeners cope with and accept feelings of loss, whereas happy music was not linked to helping with the process of grief. Dr. Van den Tol said, "Sadness often involves emotional loss, which is not a problem which can be solved or reversed. The only real way to move on and feel better is by accepting the situation and we found that people were able to do this by listening to sad music, but not so much by listening to happy music."

Right after Peter died, when I heard a song about loss, I was reduced to nonstop crying. If I heard James Taylor's song "Fire and Rain," I hit the floor in a mess of tissues and heaving sobs. If I heard a song from

A Chorus Line, which was Peter's favorite show, I instantly dissolved into a wet puddle. His favorite song was "Dance: Ten; Looks: Three," a.k.a. "Tits and Ass." I hear that, and I am in a puddle. It's weird how even tits can make me sad.

As I progressed in my journey of grief, I discovered that listening to certain songs took me to a new place of healing. Those who have had a significant loss often keep a grief playlist in their head. Each is personal and can be inspired by a memory of a song the person has heard with a loved one. We know that the pain of grief comes from feeling isolated and separated from those we have lost. Creating a grief playlist can dissolve that sense of isolation and help us find a way to heal.

If I were to find a grief playlist that would keep me moving forward in my trek through grief, it would be a mixed bag of music. I would start with Bach's Brandenburg Concertos, which make my blood pressure instantly plummet. If I am in a particularly down mood, I go to Mark Ronson's "Uptown Funk." Sometimes, I just need a bit of pepping up. Peter hated rock music and pretty much anything the grandkids played. Some of these songs are on my safe playlists, including Avicii's "Wake Me Up," (my current ringtone, denoting my nightmare, I guess), Queen's "We Will Rock You," and from *Wicked*, "Defying Gravity." I told you it was eclectic! By the way, Peter worked out to "Yackety Yak," "Roll Over Beethoven," "Love Potion Number Nine," and "Rock Around the Clock." Fifties rock and roll is now on the endangered list, so I avoid these tunes in favor of the score of *Hamilton*. Peter never got to enjoy the music of *Hamilton*, but I know he would have adored every song.

Before Peter died I couldn't listen to Sarah McLachlan's "I Will Remember You" without tearing up. Now you would have to call the paramedics! Leonard Cohen's "Hallelujah" puts me into grief bursts. Rodgers and Hammerstein's "You'll Never Walk Alone" is a killer, as is John Lennon's "Imagine." I can't listen to these evocative tunes without phoning a friend, but I am working on finding my own music to help me heal. Some tunes will uplift, and some will make me sorrowful. But I know in my heart that listening to music will help me to move forward on my journey through grief.

LAURIE'S RECOMMENDED PLAYLIST FOR GRIEVERS

"Tears in Heaven" by Eric Clapton

"Let It Be" by the Beatles

"I'll Be Seeing You" by Sammy Fain

"What I Did for Love" from *A Chorus Line*
by Marvin Hamlisch

"Without You" from *Rent* by Jonathan Larson

"Lean on Me" by Bill Withers

"Hakuna Matata" from *The Lion King*
by Elton John and Tim Rice

"My Heart Will Go On" by James Horner
and Will Jennings

"Somewhere Over the Rainbow" by Harold Arlen
and Yip Harburg

"Time after Time," Frank Sinatra's version of the song
by Sammy Cahn and Jule Styne

"Into the Fire" by Bruce Springsteen

"No One Is Alone" from *Into the Woods*
by Stephen Sondheim

I simply must end on Nat King Cole's version of "Smile," which always makes me, uh, smile!

"Smile" by John Turner and Geoffrey Parsons

Smile though your heart is aching
Smile when your heart is breaking
When there are clouds in the sky, you'll get by
If you smile through your fear and sorrow
Smile and maybe tomorrow
You'll see the sun come shining through for you

Light up your face with gladness
Hide every trace of sadness
Although a tear may be ever so near
That's the time you must keep on trying
Smile, what's the use of crying?
You'll find that life is still worthwhile
If you just smile
That's the time you must keep on trying
Smile, what's the use of crying?
You'll find that life is still worthwhile
If you just smile.

THE MYTH OF CLOSURE
The Marker Date of My Love's Death

AS I APPROACHED THE one-year anniversary of Peter's death, I tried to figure out why this date had such power over me. Anniversary dates should hold no more power over us than we are willing to cede to them. I was utterly dreading this day, but I knew I would face it head on, just as I had faced all the other rites of passage this year. An anniversary usually evokes happy events. I don't like the term "anniversary" for a death, which is filled with sadness. I have decided to call this date the "marker date" of Peter's death, which diminishes some of its significance. An anniversary connotes a celebratory situation. I didn't want to celebrate the day Peter died. I just wanted to mark it off and get on. I wanted to say, "Day done; box checked!"

I understood that I had to formulate a solid plan, plus a backup as well. I didn't want the date to sneak up on me, so I prepared to the max. My friends and support group provided a safety net and fallback system, since I really thought I might fall backward!

My son Nick and I talked about how we would commemorate this date. Nick suggested that we celebrate the fact that we survived a year without Peter. I was down with that. I could handle patting ourselves on the back for making it through the toughest year of our lives. It would be a graduation ceremony of sorts for us. We had passed all the holidays and significant reminder dates and survived. This was a major accomplishment!

There are expectations that the one-year passage is a symbol of moving on. I have learned that grief is not like a container of milk. It has no expiration date. There is no specific time when we need to be done with it or toss it into the trash. It seems that grief may have a shelf life similar to a Twinkie! The myth of closure includes the belief that after one year of grief, poof, you will magically be happy. I loved Peter for more than forty-eight years. This almost half century of love couldn't be gotten over in a year!

Getting a tattoo helped to constantly remind me of my love. I considered a few other ideas to commemorate the marker date. I was contemplating writing a letter to Peter about my survival, but I had done that to death (OK, gallows humor, I know), so I scrapped that notion. I could make Peter's favorite food, steak and fries, but that would kill me—yes, more puns. In anticipation of the marker date, I decided to see my grief therapist and cry for a solid hour, which sounds disturbing but actually made me feel a whole lot better. Yes, it would be like hitting my head against a wall, with a blessed relief after. She would take me through some guided imagery, and I would remember Peter through unconscious thoughts, which could help calm my psyche. I might bring in a candle or a helium balloon filled with a message, "You would be so proud of me, Petey," which I could release after.

On Monday, August 1, 2016, one year to the day after Peter died, I fortified my psyche with my intended plans so that I would not be surprised by my volatile emotions. I scheduled a long walk with a girl-friend, a lunch at the beach with two friends, and dinner with my son and daughter-in-law at night. I assumed I was prepared for the day. I was armed with plans, plans, and more plans. I was ready to tackle the one-year marker of the day Peter died. Bring it on!

But, what I didn't expect was that a few days before, I plummeted from a high perch of salutary tranquility into an abyss of sorrow. It hit me with such a vengeance that I was sucker-punched in the gut. It started on Friday night when I became a little weepy and began to ask the old "Why me?" unanswerable questions. "Where are you, Peter, when I need you?" Or "Why aren't you here by my side?" Or the "I miss you so much it hurts" sobbing routine. I was definitely not geared up for this behavior. By Saturday, I was a weeping mass of wet tissues, and by Sunday, I was on the floor in a puddle. Just when I thought I was hitting my stride toward my new existence, wham, I got whacked with a sorrow so deep and cavernous, I had trouble finding my way to the surface to breathe. I summoned the doctor in me and administered two glasses of sauvignon blanc before bed.

By the morning of the marker day, I was sanguine about the situation. The weekend had been tough enough, but now I faced the "terrible, horrible, no good, very bad day." I took a long walk with my friend and then readied myself to see my grief therapist. She is an amazingly kind and caring woman. I appreciate that I would not be this far in my journey were it not for this spectacularly sensitive and wise grief therapist. She has coaxed me to test the waters and try new forms of therapy to help in my process. She knew the marker day was tough for me, and she let me chatter a bit, meander, and do my usual end run to avoid the pain.

But I did face the pain head on. She had me relax and asked me where I was. I told her I was in the hospital after Peter died. I told her the doctors had asked me if I wanted to say good-bye to him. I didn't want to see him with all the tubes, but I was too weak and wrung out to resist. I told her I remembered seeing him, screaming, and falling to my knees keening and wailing. I felt her with me right there, and she suggested to me that I hadn't fallen, that I was in a supplicating position. Both of us were well aware that I am not a religious person, but it was then that I saw that I was almost praying and that I could now allow Peter to let go. I saw the tubes fall away, and I had an image of the ceiling opening, and the goodness of Peter was levitating and flying away. I was ridding myself of the horrific image of him that had been so compromised, and I was replacing it with a feeling that I was letting him go to some strange stratosphere. I began to sob uncontrollably with sorrow and paradoxically an unknown form of release. I was shocked at how I had allowed myself to redraw an image in my brain and find peace in the knowledge that the goodness in Peter was still in my heart and had been released into the arms of eternity. I was totally spent, with puffballs for eyes, but I was surprisingly aware I had discovered something that would help in the redefinition of my life.

I met two friends for lunch. Coincidentally we were all dressed in black and white, like a trio of penguin nuns. We drove to the Malibu Pier and had lunch overlooking the water. I had originally wanted to throw rocks in the ocean, but instead, I took out a pen and hurled it into the ocean, saying, "Peter, you would be so proud of my writing."

That evening my son and daughter-in-law and I consumed all the carbs we could in Peter's honor. I had made it through the first year. Check that box, Laurie!

Although that horrendous year has passed, my writing, which comforts and heals my soul, will continue for my sake and for the sake of others out there living this unspeakable journey of grief. It seems I am in this for the long haul. The acute pain has worn off, the tears have lessened, but I still wake up each day with a hollow emptiness in my heart. I have accepted my loss, I am redefining the course of my life, and writing is my purpose toward a goal of contribution. Every day I will get up knowing that I am missing Peter in my life. It will hurt, but I now have hope that, in a few years, it will hurt a whole lot less. That is a goal I can envision.

In this second year in my journey of grief, I will try to adapt to life without Peter. I know that I will be lonelier, as my support system backs off and I tire of the struggle and ergo lose courage in my passage through grief. The first year I patted myself on the back for handling the finances and for surviving an unimaginable nightmare come true. But there is something empowering about making it through that year. I know this second year will be an extreme challenge, but I have vowed to find something that I can genuinely look forward to with anticipation. Anticipation is a noun that has eluded me for a complete year. I will find a way to incorporate the yearning for Peter and make it part of my soul, integrating Peter's heart into mine. Maybe, if he is in my heart, we can beat as one again in spirit, even if he is not palpably present.

THINGS TO PREPARE FOR THE MARKER DATE

➡ Consider the marker date as a rite of passage or a turning point in your process of grief.

➡ Don't allow the date to sneak up on you. Plan ahead and have a backup plan just in case.

➡ The Jews have a one-year ceremony where a Yahrzeit candle is burned for twenty-four hours prior to the date. Yahrzeit candles are available at your local supermarket and can be burned on the marker date as a symbol of remembrance.

➡ Write a letter to your loved one telling him or her how you are coping.

➡ Sit around looking at old photos with family and friends and telling stories about your loved one. Make the stories funny!

➡ Host a dinner party for family and friends and drink a toast.

➡ Visit a favorite spot where you were together.

➡ Make a donation in your loved one's honor.

➡ Cook your love's favorite foods. For me it would be steamed lobster and corn, and I have no problem with that!

➡ Take a trip where the two of you loved to be.

➡ Have a massage!

➡ Distract yourself and go to the movies.

➡ Plant a tree in his or her honor.

➡ Set up a scholarship in his or her name.

YEAR TWO

THE SECOND-YEAR SLUMP
The Struggle to Find a New Life

EVER SINCE I PASSED the marker date of Peter's death, I have been in a funk. It didn't help that a chair had the audacity to run into me and break my toe. OK, truth be told, I ran into a chair while rushing to answer a phone. I know, I know, I shouldn't run for a phone, or as Mel Brooks says in *The 2000 Year Old Man*, "Don't run for a bus; there'll always be another…" The pain in my foot jolted me into the realization that I was truly alone and now had to find a way to heal myself physically and emotionally.

In the first year of my grief, I was pretty much running numb. I trudged along, going through significant holidays and marker dates, while trying to keep my head afloat without falling into a heap of sorrow. Year one was all about me. I dub the first year *La Bohème*, in honor of the character Mimi from my favorite opera. My biggest concerns were about me! Would I get through the year? Could I take over the finances? Could I handle the loneliness? Would I have any friends left after all my crying and blogging? It seems indeed I do. My friends have been loyal and steadfast and kind and are still my go-to posse when I need comfort. The first year seemed like some sort of test, and then after I passed the test, Peter would come back, and we would resume our life. The joke's over, you can come back now is a fantasy. This is not an exercise or a test. This is the real thing, and I still yearn for him and my life that was. Year one was a struggle for survival. Year two is about the struggle to begin to live again.

But, the second year brings up a powerful melancholy with the distinct realization that it is time to face Peter's loss head on, and more importantly,

I must tackle the loss of the life we shared together. This is where the second-year slump comes in. The numbness has worn off, and I am distinctly aware that I can no longer share my life with my love. The pain has definitely eased, but I still succumb to grief bursts, particularly on the weekends on my sad Saturdays and even sadder Sundays. Those are the days when Peter and I enjoyed so many relaxing fun times, and those are the days that pain me the most. Year two is also the pits because the world has moved on and I haven't. Life moves on as friends celebrate new milestones, new life comes into the world, and my grandkids continue to grow like weeds and almost tower over me at fifteen and eleven! All of this continues while I am barely trying to put one foot in front of the other.

These past few weeks, I have fallen into deep holes where it takes all my strength to forge forward. I get that this second year will be a tough haul. My latest funk was triggered in a doctor's office when I was filling out paperwork. I got to the status bar line that stated, "single, married," and, yeah, you guessed it, "widowed." Tears streamed down my face, and I couldn't stop sobbing. I didn't berate myself for crying; I just let it out until a release came and I could continue to take care of myself.

Hope is my aspiration. I have to find a way to anticipate good things in my life and have possibilities for a sunnier future. I can't be dependent on my son and his family. I must sign my own declaration of independence. Right now, looking ahead is too scary, but I have to find a way to see hope without fear. I know I will fall, but I also am keenly aware that I have the power to fight my way out of the abyss slowly and steadily, one step at a time. I am not Rocky Balboa, but I am a fighter who doesn't want to be mired down in grief. I will take comfort in my determination to find courage and a new life for myself. It is a small victory, but it is a victory, steeped in the promise of hope.

In this second year, I have set up some new guidelines for my healing. I hope if I follow these tenets, I will be able to see a clearer light glimmering at the end of my journey.

➡ I will make a choice to survive.

➡ I will try to find a life without Peter that has some joy. Having more sleepovers with the grandkids is a great start.

➡ I will face the feelings and emotions of grief head on, even though it sucks!

➡ When I am stressed, I will take a time out to breathe and try to see life from all perspectives. Hmm…could I be wrong? What a concept!

➡ If people cut me off in traffic, I will not give them the finger. I will remind myself that I have done the same thing on many an occasion and start laughing.

➡ I will do what kept my marriage of forty-seven years blissfully happy. I will say "my bad."

➡ I will not wait for others to call me. I will reach out to make dates with friends and family.

➡ I will exercise regularly to keep my stress levels down. Since I actually like exercise, this is not a hardship. For Peter, exercise was literally a pain!

➡ I will indulge myself in retail therapy, without the help of my dear departed Loehmann's, although Gilt.com easily helps assuage this pain.

➡ I will eat carbs when I am blue, and when I am not blue. There is nothing more healing than a bowl of my pasta à la risotto.

PASTA À LA RISOTTO
SERVES: 4–6

Cookbook author Mark Bittman came up with a fantastic idea to cook pasta like risotto and turn it into a wonderful comfort-food-like entrée. This lightened and enhanced version is amazingly delicious and easy to prepare, and it can be varied according to what produce is fresh and in season. I use gemelli pasta, named for the Italian word for twins, referring to the two strands of spaghetti that are twisted together. If you can't find gemelli, penne or mostaccioli can be substituted.

6-7 cups homemade stock or low-sodium,
fat-free chicken or vegetable stock
1 tablespoon olive oil
1 medium onion, finely chopped
2 ounces finely chopped prosciutto
1 clove garlic, finely minced
1 pound gemelli pasta
1 pound asparagus, tough stems removed, remaining
stems peeled and cut into 2-inch pieces, tips
reserved separately
salt and freshly ground white pepper to taste
1 tablespoon unsalted butter, diced
1 cup freshly grated Parmesan cheese

1. Heat the stock in a saucepan.
2. In a large nonstick deep saucepan or Dutch oven, heat the oil and sauté the onion and prosciutto over medium-high heat, stirring often for 4 to 5 minutes. Add the garlic and stir for 30 seconds to just coat with the sauce. Add the pasta and continue to cook, until the pasta is beginning to brown.
3. Ladle a few cups of the stock into the pan and continue to cook the pasta, adding more stock as it is absorbed, for about 5 minutes. Add the asparagus stems and continue to cook for an additional 5 minutes. Add the tips and cook, stirring often and adding more stock until the pasta is tender, about 3 to 5 minutes longer. There may still be a little liquid, but it will be thickened enough to have a saucy consistency.
4. Season with the salt and pepper, stir in the butter and cheese, and serve immediately in soup bowls or pasta plates.

RECALIBRATING YOUR GRIEF
My Grieving Toolbox

WHEN I FIRST BECAME a widow, I was stuck in the wilderness of grief. All the old pathways were destroyed, the signposts were gone, the bridges to happiness had collapsed, and all the roads were dead-ends to nowhere. I had to re-draw the maps and recalibrate my guide to restoration.

Recalibration is not an easy task. You need to find the tools to move forward. My grief toolbox was an odd assortment of useful devices and people that kept me going on my path towards restoration.

LAURIE'S GRIEF TOOLBOX

➡ Be supplied with as many boxes of aloe-laced tissues as possible. Costco was a great source for this item. Besides, Costco is a welcome diversion and great source of rack of lamb and good vino!

➡ Walking and exercise are great outlets for stress. Walking with a pal is preferable. Walking with a group, even better. If you don't have bad knees, running is pretty great too.

➡ Writing. I like to use my computer. I have a favorite font, Calibri, and write down my thoughts which comfort me immensely.

➡ A journal is an awesome tool to have if you don't like to write on a computer. Also, I enjoy going to

Staples or Office Depot and trying out new types of pens and paper. I think this harks back to fond memories of the first day of school and new notebooks. Too weird? I think not.

➡ Friends are a key tool in my arsenal. To quote Bette Midler, "But you got to have friends. The feeling's oh so strong. You got to have friends. To make that day last long." My friends have been loyal, steadfast, brave, truthful and yes, all the other boy scout motto stuff.

➡ Family support is key. I rest my case.

➡ It is important to see a grief therapist in the month right after your loss. I could not have forged ahead without the wonderful therapist I found at a local grief center. She sat, listened, and comforted in a way that friends could not.

➡ Joining a group is essential. Three months after Peter died, I joined a group and it was the safest place for me to grieve with like-minded, similarly-wounded grievers trying to find new pathways to forge ahead.

➡ Teach people to stop saying "pass" and tell it like it is. Euphemisms are no good in grief. He or she died. To quote Monty Python in *The Dead Parrot* sketch, the parrot is: "deceased, demised, has passed on, ceased to be, expired, gone to meet its maker, is late, bereft of life, rests in peace, is pushing up daisies, rung down the curtain, and joined the choir invisible. It is an ex-parrot!"

➡ Instruct others who want to comfort you to avoid clichés: "He's in a better place," "everything happens for a reason," and "time heals all wounds" should be dead and buried! Tell others to just sit and listen and give you a much-needed hug.

➡ Meditation is a great tool that I tend to avoid.
I recommend it to all but I just can't seem to get
into it. My form of meditation is writing. That
is the way I release my breath and relax my spirit
with words.

➡ Grief books were my salvation. I devoured book
after book on the subject of loss looking for answers
that I knew wouldn't come. The process of reading
the books, and looking for the answers, became an
invaluable part of my journey in grief. I gleaned
knowledge from experts and those who had gone
before me. The wisdom I gained became an incalculable form of comfort.

THE ULTIMATE SURVIVAL GUIDE
FOR NEW WIDOWS

WHEN PETER DIED, I had to face the practical aspects of living alone. I had to change light bulbs, hang pictures, and open jars by myself. Below is my list of key items for widows to keep on hand to make their lives easier.

➡ A secure stepladder: A woman who lives alone surely needs a secure stepladder. Invest wisely and use your coupons at Bed Bath & Beyond to get the top-of-the-line ladder. Be honest. How many times have you stepped on a chair instead of a stepladder and almost taken a nose dive? More than once, I bet! Be safe, please!

➡ Tap lights: I live in Los Angeles, where earthquakes are common, so I always keep a tap light in every room of the house in case of a power outage. They also double as great toddler toys.

➡ An electric screwdriver: This item is a must for every household but is particularly helpful for single women. Color me so proud. I just put my new license plates on my car by myself with this nifty little sucker.

➡ EZ Moves Furniture Moving System: **ezmoves.com**. When you have to move heavy furniture, simply lift, place, and slide the item. It's a dolly that doesn't take up space and can be used for a variety of household chores. OK, it doesn't help with my bad back, but just think how you can keep your chiropractor in business. (In the interest of truth, I have never used it, but it does look great in my garage.)

➡ A rubber jar opener: I love the rubber-disc jar openers, which work easily to not only open jars but to hold on to tools tightly when doing chores.

➡ Powerful flashlights: Tap-on lights work well, but you will surely need a powerful flashlight in power outages.

➡ An easy corkscrew: Invest in a self-pulling cork-screw, designed to glide smoothly through corks, with arms that extract the cork when pulled down. Or better yet, order one of the new electric cork-screws online which are a cinch to use. We have to have our vino, ladies!

➡ Spinner suitcases: These suitcases are the easiest way to whip through an airport without breaking a sweat! There are deals to be had at Costco and Target on some lightweight ones. I wish I could do carry-on, but I just can't. I live by the slogan "an item left at home is not a worthy item." At least I invested in a medium-sized lightweight spinner.

➡ Key hider: If you forget your keys, always keep one available in a very, very well-hidden place. BTW, those key hiders that look like a mound of dirt make robbers laugh!

➡ Camera surveillance system: It's costly, but I like the safety features. I have an app that tells me when a package is in front of my door. I can text my neighbor to take it in for me, making my house more secure.

Here are a few other safety tips and ideas:

➡ If you have an iPhone, the phone comes with a health app that gives you information on your heart rate, burned calories, blood sugar, and all that data. It also has a medical ID, where you fill in your medications, your emergency contact, your blood type, your weight, and your height. If you are in an accident, an EMT knows to go to your locked screen, swipe, and hit emergency. You have to set it up as "view in locked screen," but this is a fantastic safety measure!

➡ I also just learned about **kitestring.io**, which I signed up for on my computer. You don't have to walk alone anymore. Now that you are without a significant other to stay on the phone with you while you walk down a sketchy street at night, you can use Kitestring. You simply punch in your emergency contacts, let it know when you're somewhere dangerous, and Kitestring will text you a little later to see if you're OK. If you don't respond, it will let your contact or your bestie know that something may be wrong.

YOU ARE STRONGER THAN YOU THINK
Attitude Is Where It's At!

There is something you must always remember.
you are braver than you believe, stronger than you seem,
and smarter than you think.
—WINNIE THE POOH

FINDING STRENGTH IN GRIEF is no easy task. You are aware that this is probably the worst thing that will befall you, but somehow you find the strength to go on. You live through the anguish of the journey and somehow realize that you can take it—and pretty much anything else that might be dealt to you on a disgusting platter of life's bad garbage. By staying in the moment, you slowly move forward, hour by hour, day by day, and month by month, until you can look back and say, "Man, I did it!"

Attitude is a key component in how you deal with grief. If you catastrophize and go into negative thoughts, asking, "What will my future hold?" it will be harder to plow ahead. Sure, we all have our moments when we peek down the road of our future and shake with dread. The best way to forge ahead is to put on some blinders to the past, and especially to the future, and move forward in the now. Finding the strength to accomplish these tasks takes great courage and hard work. Taking breaks to exercise, eat well, and find enjoyment in day-to-day activities is key.

Resilience is the process of adapting to life in the face of adversity, trauma, or stress. It is the process of bouncing back or, as I say, bouncing forward. Resilience is an ordinary activity, not an extraordinary one. It is not a trait that people are born with. Resilience is developed through positive thoughts and actions. If you keep a positive view of your abilities and keep things in some form of perspective, even when life is throwing you the mother of all curveballs, you can persevere.

Knowing that we will most likely recover doesn't lessen the blow of immense grief. But knowing that our fears won't cripple us totally, and seeing our progress on a daily basis, can help us to find our strength. Yes, grief makes us scared, terrified, and anxious to the max. But if we can just stop every few days and take a measure of where we are in our journey, and how far we have come, the progress we have made will toughen our resolve to keep going. It is like the story of the exhausted bird who takes a breather on the branch of a tree. A strong wind suddenly blows the branch so hard that it seems as if it will break. But the bird is cool with this because she knows that she holds the power to use her wings to fly away. She also knows there are other branches on which she can rest along her travels.

In my journey of grief, I realize that I have developed the strength in my wings to fly on my own. I also am deeply aware that my friends and family are there to support me on other branches, should I falter.

A bird sitting on a tree is never afraid of the branch breaking,
because her trust is not on the branch but on its own wings.
Always believe in yourself.
—UNKNOWN

ACCENTUATE THE POSITIVE
Affirmations to Help with Grief

AFFIRMATIONS ARE POSITIVE THOUGHTS or expressions said with the express purpose of altering your thinking processes. It is a way to "accentuate the positive, eliminate the negative, and latch on to the affirmative," with thanks to lyricist Johnny Mercer. When Peter died, I needed to find something encouraging to use as a mantra, to help me move forward. Sometimes, I used humor, as is my habit, and sometimes, I used whatever crumb of gratitude I could find before me to help me find a more optimistic attitude to cope with my grief. Instead of saying, "I will never be happy again," I might say, "If I work through my grief, maybe I can find some peace and happiness in my future."

I recommend finding a quiet spot and listing a few things that come to mind. Be peaceful, and then add more ideas as you think of them during the day. Take time to customize your affirmations and post them around the house if you need. Here are a few ideas to help you get started:

→ I am finding strength in myself as I grieve.

→ I exorcize the belief that I will never recover from this loneliness. Bye-bye and good riddance to that stupid idea!

→ I absolve myself from all guilt, except for downing a pint of chocolate ice cream.

➡ I forgive myself for not being perfect. (Now this one is hard!)

➡ I am learning to heal my inner child and make her feel that she has not been abandoned.

➡ I know that it is great to see an end to my journey of grief, but in the end, it is the journey that matters.

➡ I am trying to be open to new ideas, with a little prodding, and am taking a lot of deep breaths.

➡ It's all about the present! I must allow myself to live fully in the present.

➡ I am forever changed. I will never be the same person, and that is OK for now. To quote the Greek philosopher Heraclitus: "No man ever steps in the same river twice, for it's not the same river and he's not the same man."

➡ When I am alone, I will remember that I am with a cool person—me!

➡ I know that my heart will ache more on anniversary dates and holidays, so I will make preparations to avoid being blindsided.

➡ I pledge to be gentle with myself as I plow through grief.

➡ I am entitled to take breaks from grief. Grief is totally exhausting, and I need to recoup to travel forward.

➡ I vow to dump all my feelings that "it shouldn't have happened to me." It did happen, it sucks, and I am coping.

➡ I am shattered, but I am not broken!

➡ I will use my voice to ask for help.

➡ I know that my support system is there for me forever! My friends are my rock.

➡ I am loved. I know it, and I treasure it.

➡ Happy memories of my husband, Peter are becoming comforting rather than upsetting.

➡ I am aware that helping others with their lives will help me to find hopefulness in my own life.

➡ I am finding gratitude by living the life my husband would have wanted me to live. I will honor our love, not my loss.

➡ Slowly but surely, I am making a new life for myself.

➡ I claim my power. I am worthy. I matter. I can do this!

➡ I choose to survive, with a nod to Gloria Gaynor!

GRIEVE AND GROW, OR GRIEVE AND GO
Different Styles of Grieving

"GOOD GRIEF" IS A term that I associate with the *Peanuts* characters, specifically Charlie Brown yelling through the caption on top of his head. Good grief is an oxymoron. How can grief be a good thing? I researched how this dichotomy of phrase came to be and found that it most likely arose in England as a polite way of saying "good Lord," which turned into "good God," and finally came to be expressed as "good grief!"

Good or not, grief is a full-time job! No matter what I do, somehow, the loss of Peter clouds my every move. On the surface, I am functioning like a pro! I have resumed all my activities at full throttle. I can be alone on weekends without a hitch. I am eating and sleeping normally. But underneath the facade, I have a deep and cavernous pit in my heart that occasionally becomes a thorn of incalculable pain. I use the word "occasionally" because the grief bursts have abated and I am finding small joys in life. But inside I still know that "my name is Laurie and I am a griever."

I am not a perpetual griever. I grieve, but I have learned to find meaning in my grief. The sensitivity I feel from my loss continues to make me question who I am and where I am going. My style of grief is "grieve and grow." Losing Peter has enhanced my ability to write and blog about my feelings. I am grieving well, (if that is not an oxymoron), and I am not stuck in my grief.

There are many who "grieve and go." This is a perfectly acceptable form of grief. Grieve-and-go people choose to move ahead and stockpile the memories of their experiences. They accept death more readily and don't need to constantly revisit the experience or glean any knowledge from it. Grieve-and-go people have said their good-byes, fulfilled their relationships, and stored the memories of those relationships in sealed bank vaults in their hearts and minds. This is normal and totally common.

I am, however, a grieve-and-grow type of person. I have internalized Peter's soul in my heart and have journeyed through a long process of grief, saying good-bye on a constant basis. I have learned to say farewell to the "us" we were. I have learned to mourn the future that could have been without dissolving into a puddle. I have learned to shore up the me that needs self-compassion to function on her own. I have shouted Peter's praises from the rooftop to honor his memory and keep it alive. I have internalized his goodness into my heart, making me a better human being and a more complete soul, even though he is not physically here. I have learned tolerance and compassion and the intuitive sense to listen to others. I have learned not to look too far ahead and to exist only in the safety of "now."

My writing keeps Peter's memory alive in me and affords me the opportunity to continually search for meaning in my loss. I know that I will continue to move forward from this seismic shock and find some kind of equilibrium in my life. It's not that the painful feelings will go away; it's just that they will become a badge of pride. I choose to grow and live my life in a way that Peter would have applauded. I can see him now, giving me a standing ovation, and it makes me cry and laugh at the same time. I will always grieve the loss of Peter because it inexplicably changed my life, not for the better, but for a better purpose.

HOW TO BE A FIFTH WHEEL
WITHOUT FEELING LIKE ONE
How to Navigate Picking Up the Check Gracefully

I LOVE MY FRIENDS. They are forever asking me out to dinner, and they always insist on treating. Yes, I have very kind and generous friends. They never make me feel that I am a third or fifth or even seventh wheel. When we double- or triple-dated as a couple, both Peter and I were part of conversations on politics, business, and, of course, the state of our health. BTW, after fifty, SOOH (state of one's health) is a hugely discussed topic. I felt comfortable talking with women as well as men unless the discussion centered on the state of one's prostate. I drew the line there. I still feel that I am valued for my contribution to a conversation even without Peter by my side. That is how I know that I have great friends, not fickle ones. These are the friends that loyally stick by me and want to help.

Recently, I decided to make a bargain with my friends. I would go out, but I wanted a check of my own. It works with many of my pals and is a step to being independent. I often ask the waiter discreetly for my very own check so I don't have to feel beholden to others. I wish more people could understand that widows want to pay their own way so they don't feel like outsiders. If they contribute, it makes them feel better about themselves. I also often repay friends by taking them out to a restaurant where I can sneak my card to the waiter in advance. Peter would love this. He was a notorious check grabber.

Going out to parties has its own quirks. Peter and I always had a sign language when we attended a party. He could never remember names, so when confronted with a couple I didn't know, he would gently nudge me, and I would shake hands, saying, "My name is Laurie. Sorry, I didn't get your name." It worked like a charm. Then there were the special signals for leaving. Peter liked to be in his jammies by nine o'clock sharp! From the moment we entered the party, he would signal me by pointing to his watch as a warning. Subtlety was not Peter's strong suit. After the first cookie was served, he would whisper in my ear, "five-minute warning." I may have teased him about this, but I was so happy to get home and cuddle at night.

I was recently at a party where I was talking to a person for more than twenty minutes who insisted on talking about herself the entire time. I mean, really. Couldn't she have just asked how I am doing? Couldn't she have taken a breath? I was stuck. I didn't have a partner to eye and wrinkle my brow at (even with Botox) as a hint to get me away from this narcissist!

Then there is the driving. Since Peter died, I have logged in more miles than I ever had on a car. I like to have my own car at a party, but when I drink, I generally Uber, which is a marvel! I just love Uber and Lyft, which could be the widow's best friend.

This reminds me of an old joke:

> A widower told his friend that he was going to be married.
>
> "Oh," said the friend, "I'm happy for you. Is she young?"
>
> "Not at all," replied the widower.
>
> "Well, is she pretty?"
>
> "No, she is definitely not pretty."
>
> His friend said, "Well, then she must be sexy?"
>
> "No way," said the widower.
>
> The friend continued: "Is she rich?"

"No," said the widower.

Exasperated, the friend said, "Then why are you marrying her?"

The man replied, "Because she drives at night."

TIPS FOR WIDOWS GOING OUT

➡ If you want to treat, go early and give your credit card to the waiter.

➡ Speak to your friends in advance and make it clear that you want to treat them for their kindnesses.

➡ Throw a few dinner parties to repay friends for dinners out.

➡ Set up an Uber or Lyft account.

A MOVIE FOR EVERY MOOD

A FEW WEEKENDS AGO, I was vacationing with my son Nick; daughter-in-law Carolyn; the grandkids, Lucas and Georgia; and their adorable rescue dog Simon, in Santa Barbara. I thoroughly relished my time with my sweet family, but it had been a particularly tough day for me emotionally. Peter and I had adored Santa Barbara, which we considered paradise. The entire family took a walk on the beach, and my son and I got very teary thinking about how Peter would have loved the day. Beach walking with a dog in Santa Barbara was always our go-to source of mindfulness. The breeze, the sun, the gulls, the visits with other pooches, the occasional dolphin in the distance, all gave us a sense of peace. Walking on the beach without Peter beside me brought back memories I was not ready to unearth.

That evening, the kids and I were looking for the perfect movie to watch. We powered through the list of Netflix and Amazon movies, looking for ones that were approved by Common Sense Media (commonsensemedia.org), a watchdog site that rates appropriate movies for kids. We searched through genres and focused on comedy. Lucas wanted a Marx Brothers movie, while Georgia requested *Beethoven* or *Clueless* for the umpteenth time. Suddenly we came upon *The Princess Bride*, and we all fist-bumped. Yes!

It has been over thirty years since William Goldman and Rob Reiner's cult classic, *The Princess Bride*, was released. Peter and I loved every frame of this romantic, witty fairy tale that appeals to everyone from age five to ninety. I actually don't trust anyone who doesn't get *The Princess Bride*. Those who understand the movie know that it is about sharing an outlook that doesn't tolerate bull#&*t or unimaginativeness. People who get the movie understand the importance of fantasy, laced with irony, sarcasm, and wit. I have been known to test people on their familiarity with this timeless masterpiece. I may casually say, "As you wish," waiting for a smile. I often abruptly utter, "Inconceivable," with a lisp, hoping someone will respond, "Never go against a Sicilian when death is on the line."

As I cuddled up with both kids under blankets watching the ROUS (rodents of unusual size), the characters scaling the "cliffs of insanity" or knowing that "she gets kidnapped, he gets killed, but it all ends up OK," the experience was somehow wonderfully comforting. Maybe it was the hugs, or the laughter, or the magical wit on the screen, but even though I achingly missed Peter, I found comfort in the restorative powers of *The Princess Bride*.

If *The Princess Bride* could give me comfort, I thought, why not explore other movies to match my moods? I surfed the Internet and found the AFI's 100 Years of Laugh and struck gold. Comedy lifts my mood and allows me to laugh, which is palliative on so many levels.

Let's face it: *Young Frankenstein* could cheer anyone up with lines like "What knockers!" or "Oh, thank you, Doctor," or "Hallo. Would you like to have a roll in the hay?" *The In-Laws* was a particular favorite of ours, with Alan Arkin and Peter Falk yelling, "Serpentine, Shel! *Serpentine!*" I also get great laughs from *Airplane*, *A Fish Called Wanda*, *Arsenic and Old Lace*, *The Jerk*, *City Slickers*, and *The Freshman*. As a matter of fact, most any of Nancy Meyers's movies, with the beautiful kitchens and interiors, are instant mood enhancers. *Father of the Bride*, *The Parent Trap*, *Holiday*, and *Something's Gotta Give* all give me two hours of smiling—which in my present state is a great thing!

Then there are the movies that allow for a good cathartic cry. It can be a slippery slope to pick a movie that allows for a solid and cleansing cry without shredding your soul. *Field of Dreams* requires a full box of tissues. *Dead Poet's Society* is a feel-good movie that allows for a good blubber fest. *Up* is sweetly sad, but you feel better after bawling your eyes out. I am not ready for *Beaches*, *Terms of Endearment*, or *Steel Magnolias*, which involve sickness and are gratuitously heart wrenching.

For the time being, when I want to be cheered up, I think I will stick with the following:

LAURIE'S FAVORITE UPLIFTING MOVIES

Any of Melissa McCarthy's movies because I love broad physical comedy. *The Heat* is hysterically funny and bawdy, which are both good for distraction purposes.

The Philadelphia Story

Annie Hall

Some Like It Hot

Enchanted April

Pretty Woman

The Producers or actually any Mel Brooks movie

Bringing Up Baby or *Holiday* or any movie with Katharine Hepburn and Cary Grant!

It Happened One Night or any movie with Clark Gable and Claudette Colbert!

Moonstruck

Big

Manhattan

Where's Poppa

Arthur

Notting Hill and pretty much any movie with Hugh Grant

A Shot in the Dark

Arsenic and Old Lace

The Jerk

City Slickers

The Freshman

Seems Like Old Times

Fletch

Private Benjamin

Something's Gotta Give, Father of the Bride, Private Benjamin (the first half only), *The Parent Trap*, or any Nancy Meyers movie

Broadcast News

Beverly Hills Cop and *Trading Places*, both good Eddie Murphy movies.

Victor Victoria and any James Garner movie— be still my heart!

Bull Durham

The In-Laws

A Fish Called Wanda

Airplane

Day at the Races or *Night at the Opera.* "I'll take three hard-boiled eggs!"

TRAVELING WITH A GAL PAL

AFTER FORTY-SEVEN YEARS OF marriage, traveling with Peter was a no-brainer. We had our routine down pat. He got the tickets online. I planned the rest. We're not talking a great division of labor here, but it worked for us. I mapped out lunches, dinners, and walks while Peter begged for naptimes. Our favorite place to visit was Santa Barbara. There is something peaceful about walking on Butterfly Beach that centered us both. We would stroll hand in hand, with the wind blowing, the ocean ebbing in and out, and our eyes on the horizon looking for a glimpse of a dolphin jumping out of the waves. We worshipped at the Zen of the Santa Barbara beaches. That was our religion. That was our meditative state. That was our sense of peace.

Since Peter died I have traveled to New York and to my college reunion. I have visited a girlfriend in Florida at New Year's, but this summer, I decided to brave Santa Barbara and go for a week with my friend Kath. It was the first time I was to visit this idyllic place Peter and I loved, without him or my family at my side. There were no tickets to buy because we were driving. We planned on taking two cars in case we wanted to branch off, and besides, we both love audio books so much, we figured we would happily read our way up from Los Angeles. (*The Marriage of Opposites* by Alice Hoffman is a treasure.)

I was quite aware it wouldn't be anything like the romantic times Peter and I had experienced, but I had some anticipation going, which these days is a very good thing. I have been walking with Kath for thirty-plus years, and I knew we would be a good fit. Even though I had some tearful moments missing Peter, I tried to find the positives in traveling with a girlfriend instead of a mate.

Kath and I woke up early, and when the tides permitted, we took a long beach walk on the sand, stopping to pet dogs and say hello. Everyone is friendly in Santa Barbara, including the canines. When the tides were not in our favor, we drove down by the bird sanctuary, parked, and walked the path to the wharf, passing by the zoo and catching glimpses of the giraffes being fed. We used a step app and clocked ourselves at thirteen thousand steps each day. Peter would have quit at a thousand steps for sure, or at least he would have kvetched after fifteen minutes! We then made ourselves fresh yogurt and fruit for a light and very satisfying breakfast. With Peter, I would have had to dangle a carrot of a full egg-and-bacon breakfast (no carrots included) to coax him into finishing the walk. Kath and I went to dinner with women friends and had remarkable meals, having no trouble putting four credit cards down on the table. It was key that Kath, or any friend with whom I might travel, loves to eat, because food is part of my DNA and I must obsess about my meals! Shopping was another activity Peter detested. Kath and I hit a few stores and even ventured to the outlet mall, which would have given Peter true nightmares. If Peter and I ever ventured to the outlet stores, I had to put him in the car after fifteen minutes, with the AC on full blast and an iPhone in his hand.

I resolved that I had to travel with someone who wouldn't keep me waiting. Kath and I both respect time, and it made our trip stress-free. We are also early risers who hit the hay early, which makes traveling a pleasure. Our mutual love of good wine didn't hurt either!

After we had walked our feet off, we had our rest hour and reveled in sharing beauty tips! I told her about my beloved Boots No. 7 serum, and she told me about her Benefit under eye concealer. I spritzed her with my Big Sexy Hair mousse, and we marched around in Velcro rollers with no one even blinking! I think my fave afternoon of the trip, after walking six miles, involved watching back-to-back Nancy Meyers movies while knitting.

Traveling has new meaning for me in my new normal. I am still not ready to venture far, but I am taking baby steps on my journey. Do they have a baby-step app?

TIPS ON TRAVELING ALONE AS A WIDOW

➡ Take a road trip first to test out your new single status.

➡ Travel with a friend who works on your time clock. If you are an on-time person, it would be best if your friend is of the same ilk.

➡ Travel with someone who also enjoys some of the things you do (e.g., love of food, love of exercise, love of shopping, or love of relaxation).

THE COLOR OF SADNESS
Feeling Blue?

I'VE ALWAYS WONDERED WHY people use the term "feeling blue" when they are sad. The color that clouded my horizons after Peter died was most certainly gray, not blue. I felt I was in a bad British mystery movie, in the midst of a gray, hazy, dense fog, and I couldn't find my way through the mist. I felt a heavy gray cloud looming overhead, about to rain on my soul with even more sadness. My moods were thick with gray, slightly tinged with a touch of red anger, as I railed at my tragedy. I know that since Peter died, I have many moments when I "feel blue," but I can't fault my favorite color for my mood.

Some attribute the phrase "feeling blue" to the tradition of ships flying blue flags and bearing a painted blue band when a captain or another officer has died. Another origin of "the blues" is derived from mysticism involving blue indigo, which was used by many West African cultures in death and bereavement ceremonies, where all the mourners' garments would have been dyed indigo to indicate suffering. This mystical association toward the indigo plant was transported to the United States by the slaves who worked on cotton in the Southern plantations, often singing dirge-like songs referred to as "the blues."

The word "blue" was first used by Chaucer in about 1385, in his poem *Complaint of Mars*. Washington Irving is credited with having first used the term "the blues" in 1807, as a synonym for sadness: "He conducted his harangue with a sigh, and I saw he was still under the influence of a whole legion of the blues." Irving was shortening the phrase "blue devils," which was a synonym dating back to Elizabethan time to describe a menacing presence. "The blues" as a musical form, featuring flattened thirds and sevenths, may have originated around 1895, although officially in W. C. Handy's "Memphis Blues."

For me, blue represents tranquility, harmony, peace, and relaxation. My house is decorated in blue and white. I don't find sadness in blue. Blue is also associated with the fifth chakra, located at the throat and therefore connected to communication. Someone who speaks the truth is "true blue." I like the color blue. It makes me see clearly and find my way in the world in a calm and coherent manner. I have vowed to continue to look at the blue horizon and avoid the gray clouds of sadness to find solace and comfort in my journey toward restoration.

Your attitude is like a box of crayons that color your world.
Constantly color your picture gray, and your picture will
always be bleak. Try adding some bright colors to the picture
by including humor, and your picture begins to lighten up.
—ALLEN KLEIN

THE COURAGE OF MY CONVICTIONS
How Widows Can Find the Courage to Move Forward

I learned that courage was not the absence of fear, but the triumph over it. The brave man is not he who does not feel afraid, but he who conquers that fear.
—NELSON MANDELA

A YEAR AND FOUR months ago, after Peter died, grief took charge of me and blazed a fiery path through my heart. Today, I can honestly say that I am in charge of grief! The sadness is profound, the hole in my heart is still cavernous, but the good news is that my heart keeps on beating. My survival is about courage. Processing grief takes immense courage. Honoring your grief takes guts, grit, determination, and about everything you can marshal in your arsenal of audacity to move forward.

When I think of courage, I think of Bert Lahr as the Cowardly Lion singing in *The Wizard of Oz*:

I'm afraid there's no denyin'
I'm just a dandy-lion
A fate I don't deserve
I'm sure I could show my prowess
Be a lion, not a mouse
If I only had the nerve.

In the movie, we witness the lion learn to find courage in self-confidence. The word "courage" comes from the French word "cœur," which means heart. Our Cowardly Lion is looking for a heart when he wants courage. We know that the lion is so ashamed of his fear and cowardice that he cannot recognize his innate courage to help Dorothy travel all the way to see the Wizard of Oz. Once he realizes his own bravery and nerve, he can finally warm to the feeling of courage.

We have heard the term "liquid courage" to describe the effects of alcohol, but those fortifying effects last only as long as the high does. Similarly, medications give you "biochemical courage" and can temporarily help you through some tough times, but ultimately you must find your own courage to honor grief and find your way through this arduous journey.

When I think of the word "courage," thoughts of bravery come to mind, like knights in shining armor rescuing damsels in distress, or firefighters saving victims. But bravery is not courage. Bravery is the daring to go forward. Courage is the quiet resolve and commitment to act bravely. I have learned to welcome courage daily. When Peter first died, it was all I could do to get out of bed. I had to pat myself on the back each day for facing the day alone. The journey through grief takes all the courage you can muster.

Grievers are a courageous bunch. Each day we must acknowledge our pain and find the strength to keep going. We are navigating a terrain with no road maps or trail markers. We have to find our own path to restoration, and it takes immense courage and fortitude. Others have traversed these paths, but it is only through our personal courage to face the journey that we can discover the direction to find our true selves again. The struggle comes when we finally realize that our loved ones are never coming home and we have to figure out how to live without them and redefine ourselves. Like the Cowardly Lion, I didn't realize how strong I had become in life, until I was called upon to be the full being that was inside me. Real courage is not the absence of fear but the motivation to move forward in spite of it. E. E. Cummings tells us, "It takes courage to grow up and become who you really are." I am using courage to find out who I truly am and to value the person I have become.

TIPS FOR WIDOWS TO FIND COURAGE IN LIFE

➡ Find gratitude in parts of your life. It can be trifling things that happen, but learn to be grateful for small favors.

➡ Celebrate who you are and how far you have come. If you journalize, you can chart your progress and applaud small victories.

➡ Have the courage to help others, which will help you in turn.

➡ Do not think of your loss as an ending but more as a change toward a new and different life.

➡ Be adventurous and try new activities, hobbies, or travels and find some joy in them.

➡ Remember that others have courageously traveled the road of grief and lived to tell the tale.

AFTERIMAGE
Loving Truly, Madly, Deeply

AN AFTERIMAGE IS A type of optical illusion in which an image continues to appear briefly even after exposure to the image has ended. If you stare for a long time at a fixed point and then shift your gaze suddenly, you might notice an afterimage, in which you still see the image you were first admiring. We all get afterimages when we stare at bright lights for a while.

After Peter died I had a clear picture of him in my brain. I could see him walk in the door at the end of the day, so pleased to be home. I could see him come down the stairs in the morning smiling; I could see him getting ready to go play golf with a wide grin on his cute face. These were sharp images in my brain, even though he was gone. But now that time has elapsed, it is as if I am looking away and only seeing the shadows of an afterimage. I am saddened that I can't see him clearly in my mind. The images that were once ingrained in my memory are fading, and I am having trouble processing this secondary loss.

There is something so wonderful about the ability to unmistakably see the afterimage of life. I am craving the images of Peter, and even though I can see him in photographs, it is not the same as seeing the sweet memories of him in my mind. I am craving the videos in my mind. I am craving the moments that used to play in my head over and over and bring a smile to my face. I want the afterimage videos back, but they are fading, and I am trying to figure out how to resurrect the memories in a keepsake chest in my head and in my heart.

In a way, I am seeing a pentimento. A pentimento is an alteration in a painting, where you see what the artist has previously added to the painting. Lillian Hellman talks about this technique in her book *Pentimento*. "Old paint on a canvas, as it ages, sometimes becomes transparent. When that happens, it is possible, in some pictures, to see the original lines: a tree will show through a woman's dress, a child makes way for a dog, a large boat is no longer on an open sea." That is called pentimento because the painter "repented," changed his or her mind. Similarly, I am seeing Peter's images in layers, and the afterimage is getting more shadowy and indistinguishable.

The other day I decided to see one of my favorite movies, *Truly, Madly, Deeply*. Anthony Minghella directed this jewel of a flick in 1990. One of my heartthrobs, the late actor Alan Rickman, plays the cellist, Jamie, who has just died. His girlfriend, Nina, played by the brilliant Juliet Stevenson, is devastated and can't get on with her life. Jamie returns in the form of a ghost, which keeps her from moving on. The point of the movie has become clear: Jamie came back specifically to help Nina get over him, by tainting her idealized memory of him.

I don't want to have to tarnish Peter's memory to move on. I want to fold the pleasurable memories into a part of my brain where they can be stored in perpetuity. I want to pause the videos of him and be able to remember all the wonderful smiles and the goodness of his nature. It is confusing and hazy, and a concept that will need my full attention to put into action. I am hoping that I will one day be able to remember my past life with Peter and integrate that fully into my new, acceptably different existence.

> *When we think of loss, we think of the loss, through death,*
> *of people we love. But loss is a far more encompassing theme in*
> *our life. For we lose not only through death, but also by leaving*
> *and being left, by changing and letting go and moving on.*
> —JUDITH VIORST

BUILDING STRENGTH AND RESILIENCE IN GRIEF

RESILIENCE IS NOT A protective shield that we put up to prevent us from pain. Resilience allows us to feel the pain, the anger, and the angst, and move through these emotions to get to the other side of grief. Resilience is about marshaling all our resources to find the energy and stamina to make it through the journey of grief. Resilience teaches us to prevent the what-ifs from creeping into our attitude. Resilience is the choice we make to put our efforts into working through grief. Resilience is our ability to bounce forward when the s*%t hits the fan.

Sheryl Sandberg and Adam Grant describe resilience best in their book *Option B*. "Resilience is the strength and speed of our response to adversity—and we can build it. It isn't about having a backbone. It's about strengthening the muscles around our backbone."

In order to develop the resiliency to work through your journey of grief, you need to reorder your brain for a more positive approach. This is no easy task when the world as you know it has collapsed around you. When you are resilient, you can view grief as a challenge, not a paralyzing event. Resilient people are committed folks with goals and energy to focus on the situation and move through it. Resilient people are optimistic and view bad events as a temporary setback rather than a permanent situation.

Resilience is ordinary, not extraordinary. Most people display resilience in the face of adversity. Resilience is not an innate trait but is more of a learned response to a situation. Resilience is a choice you must make. Making the choice to be resilient can restore a sense of control and thus make you feel stronger. To develop resilience in grief, you have to make a conscious effort to find the energy to forge ahead with the use of a few tools:

➡ Maintaining a positive outlook of yourself. Self-compassion and the ability to forgive yourself are integral parts of resilience. Do not tackle this in the middle of the night! Best to wait until after breakfast when things look a bit more hopeful.

➡ Taking good care of yourself, physically and emotionally. You need to have enough sleep, food, and exercise to find the strength to work through grief. Try to avoid the ice cream and cookie binges in the middle of the night, although an occasional sweet splurge is sometimes a necessity. Has anyone tried Bart & Judy's chocolate chip cookies? Yum.

➡ Fostering good relationships with family and friends. If you are willing to ask for help or even just accept help, you are well on your way to resiliency. Your friends and family are your safety net. Dump toxic friends which will do wonders for your psyche.

➡ Altering your view of hardship as surmountable, rather than overwhelming, will help to build resiliency. Think of "The Little Engine That Could," and allow "I think I can" to be your new mantra.

➡ Clocking your growth. Be willing to look back at your progress and applaud your victories, even if they are tiny. You are stronger than you think.

➡ Keeping things in perspective. In *Man's Search for Meaning*, Viktor Frankl put his experience in a concentration camp into perspective so he could survive the horrors of war.

➡ Allowing yourself the space to experience emotions. But if they are too painful, allow yourself the comfort of rest until you are ready. Cry in the shower or in the car. You can actually feel better although it does wreak havoc on your eyes!

➡ Pacing yourself. This is a slow and steady race, and you need to build up your strength gradually. Don't think you have to recover overnight. Grief takes time and work and yes, resilience!

➡ Being helpful to others. This will reset your moral compass and make you feel better about yourself. Volunteer big time!

➡ Using humor and laughter as breaks to build resilience. "It could work" from Young Frankenstein is my motto.

➡ Developing the ability to feel gratitude again despite the loss of our love. This is a hard one. Find enjoyment in a bag of popcorn, a good movie, or a good movie with a bag of popcorn!

➡ Asking ourselves if negative thoughts and actions help or hinder our journey through grief. If we try to move negative thoughts to the back of our minds, it can help us to gain a positive attitude. This is not an easy task but when you take the time to look at where your head is, this in itself is a positive step.

➡ Developing private rituals for mourning. Play a song, watch a movie, look through photo albums, or light a candle in your loved one's honor. Rituals help you find the control to move forward. Walking is a way I can get closer to Peter and almost hear his voice advising me to be resilient!

~~~~~~

BUSTING THE MYTHS OF GRIEF

I AM FED UP with grief myths—those false expectations and misjudgments that make grief recovery even harder. I have compiled a list of fifteen grief myths that I am exposing. I would love to hear from you about what grief myths bother you.

> **MYTH:** Grief and mourning are the same.
> **REALITY:** Grief is your own personal response to a loss. It's the numbness, sadness, anger, and regret, all rolled into one. It's the pain in your gut and hole in your chest. Mourning is the act of expressing your grief and releasing it by crying, talking about the death, writing, or even punching a pillow!
>
> **MYTH:** The first year of grief is the hardest.
> **REALITY:** The first year is extremely difficult to navigate, but the loneliness of the second year can be just as painful.
>
> **MYTH:** Tears are a sign of weakness.
> **REALITY:** Not only is crying normal, but it is a necessary release. Emotional tears have been shown to have a palliative and calming effect.
>
> **MYTH:** Grief occurs in predictable stages.
> **REALITY:** Grief is individual and unique. Grief reflects the nature of the relationships we had with our loved ones, the ways the deaths occurred, the

support systems we have in place, and our cultural and religious backgrounds.

MYTH: Grief has a shelf life.
REALITY: Grief lasts forever. When we love this deeply, the loss is always in our hearts. Grief becomes less intense and more adaptable, but it is still with us, and we will mourn the loss eternally.

MYTH: Time heals all wounds.
REALITY: I believe that time heals wounds to some degree, but the scars of pain are left in our hearts to remind us of what we have been through and survived.

MYTH: Keeping busy will make grief easier.
REALITY: You can't put off the journey of grief. You can run around and keep busy, but eventually you have to look grief in the face and deal with it head on!

MYTH: Grief offers closure.
REALITY: Closure is for business deals, not grief. Grief helps us heal the wounds of heartbreak. We can be mindful, we can exercise, we can journalize, but they only offer healing properties. We can't tie up our emotions with a neat bow and call this process closed. Grief is a lifelong journey.

MYTH: The purpose of grief is to get over it.
REALITY: I will never get over the loss of Peter.
As time goes by and the intense pain eases,
I will adapt to my new life, but Peter is still imprinted, ever so comfortably, inside the chambers of my heart.

MYTH: If someone looks OK, that person is done with grief.
REALITY: Grievers resent people telling us we look OK, as if that will make it all go away. We may look hot on the outside, but on the inside, we are still grieving deeply.

MYTH: If you keep a stiff upper lip, à la Jackie Kennedy, you will get through the process of grief more easily.
REALITY: Being stoic is not a smart choice when grieving. It takes extreme courage and emotion to grieve. I had to let out all my feelings in order to move forward.

MYTH: Grief is the same as sadness.
REALITY: Grief is sadness to the nth degree. Sadness is a part of grief.

MYTH: The goal of grief is to let go of your loved one and move on with life.
REALITY: Fuggedaboutit! I will never let go of Peter's memory and our love. It will not stop me from moving on, but I was married to Peter for a long time, and he is part of my soul, and he continues to make me a better person.

MYTH: Dating means you are not loyal to your loved one who died.
REALITY: Peter would be the first one to tell me to get out there and date! Of course, he would have been horrified at the schlubs on the dating websites!

MYTH: If you still display photos of your loved one, you are stuck.
REALITY: It is important to have pictures of your loved one around. I still find it hard to look at pictures of Peter without welling up with tears. My goal is to be able to look at them and smile. I am not stuck; I am grieving.

THE ART OF NOW
How to Stay in the Present

BEFORE PETER DIED I was the planner in the family. I scheduled dinners with couples, I gave parties, and I planned trips. The trips were elaborately arranged down to the minute. We toured museums, visited friends in the East, and were constantly on the go when we traveled. I reveled in planning. I enjoyed mapping out the tiniest details. I relished being the architect of our lives. Peter never minded a second of my planning. He loved following the program, except when it involved hiking or too much walking. I always made a point to add a naptime to our schedule to make him content. I used to ask Peter, "When did you lose control in this relationship?" He always laughed and said, "Do the words 'I do' strike a familiar note?"

There were times when we let the present slip away, rushing past to get to the next thing while squandering precious moments. Basically, we made it a house rule to live each moment to the fullest. I distinctly remember feeling, "I want this moment to last forever." I was present, and he was present, and even if we planned too much, we made the most of every second. Toward the end of Peter's life, he said, "If I die tomorrow, I will have no regrets." He meant every second of this statement. He loved his friends, his family, and especially his grandkids. After picking them up at school, he would tell me stories of each blissful moment and relish in the tales. This was our state of mindful coupleness. We trusted in our relationship and therefore respected each other's space and the space we shared. That's how we made it work for forty-seven years.

When Peter died I no longer wanted to plan. I couldn't look back at my memories. I couldn't look to the future. It all seemed bleak. Grief takes you out of the past and away from the future and slams you into the present. It is only in the present that you can find some small victory, so you can wake up the next day. It is only in the present where you can feel the loss and notice that maybe you haven't cried as much today. It is only in the present that you can find joy in a meal, in a movie, in a song, in a child.

I am now living moment to moment in my soul. I have to trust in the process of my journey toward adapting to my new life. I have to let my heart lead me, and stay out of my head. I am trying to savor the moments with the grandkids. Recently, I had them stay over for a long weekend, and I enjoyed every second without fretting over what would happen next. I took them to the movies, I took them to mouth-watering sushi dinners, and I took them bowling. I smartly had each child bring a friend so I didn't have to bowl and throw my back out. Have any of you been bowling recently? Who knew one and a half hours of three games for four kids would cost $130? I mindfully accepted the cost, which brought me back to the present and the fun I had watching the kids laugh. Thank goodness for the new bumpers in bowling alleys!

My mindful way of healing is through writing. When I am writing at my computer, I am in such a state of total absorption, known as *flow*, that I often lose track of time. My writing is my way of staying in the present, and pouring my heart out to Peter and to the universe. I am trying to release the pain by living it and moving forward. I have to accept the feelings, cry, and let them come out on the paper. It is through writing that I feel a sense of accomplishment, even if it is just stream of consciousness.

I do not want mindfulness to be a goal because goals are about the future. I just want to have an intention to live in the present. I still can't meditate on my own. I can contemplate with my therapist in a safe haven. I can openly and safely share my pain with my support group. I know that I can't meditate alone yet because when I do I strip all my protective gear away, and I am wracked with heaving sobs. For now, I will be mindful of my writing and call that a miniature victory.

If you are depressed
you are living in the past.
If you are anxious
you are living in the future.
If you are at peace
you are living in the present.
—LAO TZU

LIMINALITY
The Threshold Betwixt and Between

THE WORD "LIMINALITY" IS derived from the Latin word "limen," meaning threshold. According to dictionary.com, "liminality is the transitional period or phase of a rite of passage, during which the participant lacks social status or rank, remains anonymous, shows obedience and humility, and follows prescribed forms of conduct, dress, etc." I can identify with liminality as I navigate through my journey of grief—without the obedience and humility verbiage, thank you very much! What was once a world I cherished and adored is now turned upside down, and I am on the threshold of Betwixt-and-Between Land. A state of liminality is one where the order of things has been suspended. It is an unsettling arena where I am learning to steer my vehicle and hoping to guide it toward finding my new self. In liminality, the past is brought into play only briefly to review the loss. It is the future and the promise of transformation that I find so heartening about liminality.

The idea of liminality was introduced into the field of anthropology in 1909 by Arnold Van Gennep in his work *Les Rites de Passage*. Van Gennep described the rites of passage, such as coming-of-age rituals and marriage, as having the following three-part structure: separation, liminal period, and reassimilation. A grieving person can be considered to be going through this pattern. The person feels the loss, then is inducted into the liminal transition period, and finally reassimilates into society. It was not until the second half of the twentieth century, with the writings of Victor Turner, that the concept of liminality was explored fully. In *Liminality and Communitas*, Turner began by defining liminal individuals as "neither here nor there; they are betwixt and between the positions assigned and arrayed by law, custom, convention, and ceremony." But Turner gives hope by referring to "betwixt and between" through the concept of the "realm of pure possibility."

When Peter died, I experienced a loss so great that I was thrown into a liminal state of uncertainty. Losing a loved one creates a void that leaves an emptiness that weighs so heavily on your heart that you have to look inward in order to move forward. Sadness catapulted me into a liminal state, forcing me to regroup and turn inside myself. Essentially, it made me take a very long emotional time out. I had to honor the pain as I would have done with a physical injury. There is no Tylenol or Advil for grief. I had to heal myself holistically while searching for my life force in this liminal space. I had to sit in this unsettling place using my core beliefs; the help and support of family and friends; daily exercise; and even my daily routines to dig into my stripped-down spiritual self and retrieve what was left of Laurie after PeterLaurie—not to be confused with the actor Peter Lorre. That was *The Way We Were*, to quote one of my favorite movies: "What's too painful to remember we simply choose to forget"…for a while.

But I have moved through this threshold now. I am looking through the door and stepping into a world that is completely altered. A year after Peter's death, I now see the space of liminality as a way to provide limitless opportunities for me in a new and transformative life. My writing has gotten me through the door and into the open air. My determination has propelled me like an Energizer bunny to keep me moving forward no matter what lies in my path. My support system constantly reminds me of who I am and how I will evolve. They cheer me on like I am a rock star. As I recover myself in my liminal state, I have hope and anticipation of what lies beyond door number one for myself, and for others who are struggling on the threshold betwixt and between a new normal.

EATING YOUR GRIEF
How to Raise the Level of Cooking for One

AFTER PETER DIED, I lost my desire to be creative in the kitchen. I went out to eat a lot but just didn't have the chops (insert cringe at pun here) to cook dinner for myself. For a food writer who concentrated on healthful cooking, it took quite a while for me to enjoy being creative in my kitchen. Before Peter died, I used to love to visit the Saturday Farmers' Market in Santa Monica and make my meal plans based on what was seasonably available. I missed that impetus to get my creative culinary juices flowing. For about eight months, I coasted on dinners that consisted of soups and comfort foods, which I occasionally prepared or bought, and kept in small containers in my freezer. The truth be told, I also ate a lot of microwave popcorn, and I would crunch away my anger and sadness.

I started to enjoy cooking again when I started to entertain. I had to repay people for their kindnesses in treating me to wonderful restaurant dinners. I started with my old standbys, like butterflied roast chicken, mustard-coated rack of lamb, turkey chili, and coq au vin. I bought pieces of salmon and tried to roast them in new ways, especially with cilantro (Peter's nemesis). I whipped up Thai chicken noodle soups using zucchini noodles prepared with my new vegetable spiralizer. I ordered truffle honey and mint jellies on Amazon and began to graduate to more sophisticated dishes.

One night, I was feeling like I needed comfort, and I remembered that Peter and I scarfed up the most amazing creamy scrambled eggs on a trip to Paris. That was a fond memory that I wanted to recreate. Fond and memory were two things that hadn't meshed together for a long time in my journey of grief, so this was a good thing. I went to YouTube and found Gordon Ramsay preparing the most amazing eggs that were destined to be my dinner and my source of comfort. I enjoyed every minute of the video and instantly decided to cook the eggs, served alongside a baguette toasted with melted butter. The results were so amazing that I do this dish every few weeks and enjoy the food and the memories I shared with Peter.

Cooking for one is often problematic for people in the throes of grief, especially those mired in complicated grief. Complicated grief is a condition in which typical second-guessing kinds of thoughts, and avoidance of trigger-provoking activities, interfere with adapting to loss. People in complicated grief can't accept the reality of their situation and struggle to adapt to a new life without their loved one. If you can't adapt to your loss, your grief stays intense and therefore becomes complicated. Dr. Katherine Shear, director of the Center for Complicated Grief at Columbia University, developed this amazingly successful sixteen-session program, which helps so many stuck in complicated grief. Dr. Shear sent me a paper by Heather Nickrand and Cara Brock, who work as bereavement coordinators with Alexian Brothers Hospice. They presented an idea for *culinary grief therapy*, which Dr. Shear knew would inspire me particularly, since I have written four cookbooks. It suddenly struck me that just the act of going to a grocery store is painful, since it was often a shared activity that triggered the memory of Peter trying to slip Krispy Kremes into the supermarket cart! Even going to restaurants can produce sad memories and surging bouts of tears. Food is love, but it is also shared love, and the loss is palpable each time I eat alone or cook alone. Nickrand and Brock started a workshop they call "Cooking for One," focusing on culinary grief therapy. The series, facilitated with the College of DuPage Culinary and Hospitality Department in Glen Ellyn, Illinois, is an interactive form of grief therapy that offers comfort to those experiencing grief. It is a variant of group therapy and teaches people how to navigate the cooking process solo.

There is also a site called The Dinner Party, Life After Loss, **thedinner party.org**, geared to twenty- to thirty-somethings who have experienced significant loss. You can "join a table" of bereaved people who meet over potluck dinners and talk about how grief affects their lives. It is matchmaking for young people journeying through grief. I love the mottos on the website: "We believe in thriving, not just surviving" and "We'll take damn good care of ourselves and of each other. We will eat well, be well, live well, love well."

I realized that sometime over the past year, I decided to do my own culinary grief therapy by once again going to the farmers' markets on a regular basis, and planning meals around seasonal foods. I organized potluck dinners and found that people wanted to contribute dishes and had a better time as a result. I doubled recipes and put small portions in the freezer. In my heart, I knew that Peter would have wanted me to be more compassionate with myself and to improve my eating habits. He used to say, "Eat, skeleton!" I decided to eat foods that made me content and that made me focus on good memories of our dinnertimes together. I began to eat more pasta, which he adored, and fish and veggies, which I loved but he abhorred. Below please find my version of the most amazing creamy soft-scrambled eggs on the face of the planet, which we both consumed with delight on weekends!

AMBROSIAL CREAMY SOFT-SCRAMBLED EGGS WITHOUT CREAM
SERVES 1 HUNGRY PERSON

For these amazing eggs, you will need a heavy-bottomed, nonstick saucepan and a silicone heat-resistant spatula. Depending on the number of eggs you are using, and the size of the pan, you must plan on at least fifteen minutes of cooking time, so make sure you have some music going to enjoy the experience.

> **3** fresh eggs
> **1** tablespoon unsalted butter
> salt and freshly ground pepper to taste
> *Garnish:* freshly snipped chives
> *Accompaniment:* toasted baguette

1. In a small bowl, whisk your eggs thoroughly until they are evenly yellow.
2. In a heavy-bottomed nonstick saucepan, place the butter and allow it to melt over low heat. Pour in the eggs and make sure the heat is very, very low.
3. Start stirring with the spatula immediately. The more you stir, the creamier the eggs will be. After about 5 minutes, you will see the custardy curds forming in the pan. Keep stirring constantly. (Note: If too many curds begin to form, remove the pan from the heat to slow down the cooking process).
4. When the eggs form wonderful creamy curds, after about 15 minutes, season them with salt and pepper, garnish with snipped chives, and serve immediately, accompanied by a toasted baguette.

TOE IN THE WATER
Back in the Dating Pool

IT HAD BEEN A year and a half since Peter died, and I was traveling to New York for a week to see friends and theater. I had met a guy at my college reunion, an actor—I know, I know—but he was six-foot three-inches tall, nice and rugged looking, and a widower. He told me that when I came to Manhattan, I should call and we could dine. I called, we made a date around his shooting schedule, and I was psyched. Toe in the water, right? My therapist told me not to take a wedding dress on the first date, and I listened.

On the day of the prearranged date, the rain was coming down like Noah's flood. I mean deluge city, so I popped in for a hair blowout. I must admit that I had butterflies in my belly. Yes, I was nervous. It had been almost half a century since I had been on a date, and things had drastically changed. Thankfully this wasn't a Tinder hookup. I guess dating morphs us back to being teenyboppers with a hell of a lot more wrinkles!

I got to the restaurant, and the guy was sitting there waiting. A good sign. I was on time, and he was early. Nice. I smiled. I sat down, and even before my butt touched the seat, he said, "I almost didn't make it. I had my fourth bout of diverticulitis this year." OK, so much for pleasantries. I smiled, looking what I thought was pretty hot, in a sheer black lace top and a fab jacket. Actor boy didn't seem to notice. He said, "Let's order." I asked if I could please get a glass of wine ASAP! The waiter, sensing my distress, came running back with the wine, and I took a long swig for courage.

211

Actor boy proceeded to order a pasta with cherry tomato sauce, and I blurted out, "It's got seeds and will make you sicker!"

He said, "You mean the tub of popcorn I ate last night wasn't good for me?"

I rolled my eyes and morphed into lay-doctor mode and told him what he shouldn't eat with diverticulitis. I strongly suggested visiting a nutritionist to learn more and prevent it from happening four times in one year. Why is it that some dudes are medical morons?

Noticing there were many pregnant pauses, I moved into Barbara Walters interview mode and started the questions. I asked him about his wife and how she died. I commiserated and told him about Peter's sudden death. Another pause, so I continued to channel my inner interviewer persona, asking questions and pushing onward through the next glass of vino and his fourth. By this time, my duck ragù pasta was virtually untouched because I didn't have time to shovel in a mouthful while continuing with my queries. Couldn't he have asked about my life at least once?

He was a kind man, but an actor, which I made note of as a group to rule out on future dates. He paid and said, "Let me walk you back to your place." He put my arm in his, which felt overwhelmingly awesome. It had been a long time since I had felt safe while walking on the arm of a very tall and attractive man. We emerged onto the street only to be hit by a monsoon. We walked the block back to where I was staying at a friend's place, and by that time my hair was dripping wet and I was soaked and shivering. He gave me a peck on the lips, and we parted as he said that when he was next in Los Angeles, he would look me up. I breathed a sigh of relief that he didn't want to come up for a nightcap. I was the same age as he, and clearly way too old for him, to the tune of twenty years.

It was a toe in the water, and I realized I could do it, but perhaps not with an actor.

I AM SICK AND TIRED OF BEING A WIDOW!

WHEN YOU ARE IN the depths of grief, you wallow for a while, then you nurture yourself, and then you move forward. But every once in a while, you have to vent and get that hurricane of pent-up anger to the surface and out! From time to time, you just have to be honest with yourself and others, and scream at the universe that you are sick of being a widow. Knowing that I am honestly spilling my guts does wonders for my well-being!

➡ I am frustrated that I have to tell my widow's story.

➡ It is hard to believe, but I am even irritated about using the "widow card" to get out of a traffic ticket! Although, I must say, the benefits outweigh my annoyance.

➡ I am pissed off that I am my own mirror. I miss Peter's admiring glances and pinches, and his touch. Hell, I miss sex. I know my son is reading this, but I can't help it. I miss sex. More than that, I genuinely miss being held.

➡ I'm disgusted with the old sleepshirts I wear because no one can see them. I put all my pretty nightgowns at the back of the closet in a box with tearstains on the top.

➡ I have relegated my fancy dresses and high heels to the back of the closet. Actually, putting away

the stilettos has helped my back immeasurably!
Move this to the plus column.

➡ I detest driving at night. I am especially annoyed
that I can only down one glass of wine at night
because I am my own designated driver. Yes, yes, I
can take Lyft or Uber, but I feel better in my own car.

➡ I miss Peter screaming at drivers as they cut
him off. I don't, however, miss him shooting
the bird at them.

➡ I am irritated that I even tried to go on a dating
site. The guy with his profile picture seated in a
Barcalounger did me in!

➡ I am sick of watching television alone. *Homeland*
makes me so nervous that I climb under the covers.
I am bothered that Peter is not here to walk me up
to bed after the show and assure me the windows
and doors are all bolted shut.

➡ I am tired of being afraid of the calendar. Holidays,
birthdays, and anniversaries loom large with
anticipatory grief.

➡ I am nauseated by my eating habits. Onion rings,
popcorn, and chocolate are not a balanced diet, or
even worthy food groups!

➡ I miss our cozy dinners together at the kitchen
table, and I am so sad that I am losing the memory
of those dinners.

➡ I am burned out trying to find the self-compassion
to love the person I have become.

➡ I am ticked off that I am so lonely.

➡ I am sad that when I am sick, I have to take care
of myself. Chicken soup in the freezer is a plus.

➡ I am so very tired of sobbing in the meat aisle
(Peter loved his New York steaks) and watching the
pitiful reaction of the butchers.

➡ I am overtaxed handling the finances, but I guess
that is not just a widow's complaint.

➡ I'm shattered when I feel so proud of my son and
my grandkids and have to share it alone without
high fives, hugs, and tears of joy with Peter.

➡ I'm annoyed that I have to travel alone and that
when the plane ride gets bumpy, I have to grip the
armrests instead of Peter and then follow up with
a bath in Purell.

➡ Even though I am tired of blogging about grief,
it is the one thing that helps me to move forward,
for which I am truly grateful. Writing cleanses
my anger and frustration and heals my soul.

To quote Elton John, "I'm still standing. Yeah, yeah, yeah."

~~~~~~

REAL MEN DON'T GRIEVE, OR DO THEY?

I WAS LUCKY ENOUGH to have a man in my support group who was open to expressing his feelings. It was gratifying to see him work through his pain without shame or stigmas attached. This is clearly not the norm. I have discovered, from other widows and widowers, that men and women handle grief in a completely different manner. Western cultural expectations allow women to mourn overtly and insist that men soldier on stoically. It seems that grief is the great emasculator. Intense loss strips us of all control and self-esteem.

Cultural expectations for men and women define the ways we grieve differently. Men are expected to be warrior-protector types who must take their intense feelings of loss and compartmentalize them into a box with a lock on it, marked "Do not open!" Since men are the "strong" ones, taboos forbid them from expressing their feelings. They must move into take-charge mode and see loss as a challenge to be conquered. Men are instrumental grievers, with a focus on overcoming their grief by use of physical or cognitive methods, moving on as quickly as possible. Men also use the Greta Garbo "I want to be alone" method of grieving. Solitude seems an easier route for them. When they do open up, it is in a storytelling style rather than the feeling style of a woman who talks candidly. Despite the fact that both men and women have tear ducts, men do not cry very often. Interestingly, studies indicate that after puberty a male produces less of the tear-producing hormone prolactin, leaving him physiologically less able to cry.

It is said that "women mourn and men replace." Since statistically widows outnumber widowers by a vast margin, widowers are pursued by the "casserole ladies," ready to provide open arms and comfort from the moment the casket is closed. Many widowers are so used to be taken care of, they find the consolation of another woman an easier road to take than mucking through the mire of grief. Most widowers end up finding relationships and remarrying very soon after their loss.

In general, men would rather be mute than talk through their grief. They feel powerless and do not want to rehash the feelings of loss. Male grief focuses on action. They want to turn into Mr. Fixit and repair their grief. They feel that expressing their grief won't bring their spouses back, so they often avoid counseling. Men feel angry, restless, and tense in grief. Women feel depressed and abandoned but understand the purpose of the grieving process to help relieve their pain. Men use this stiff-upper-lip approach which becomes totally imprudent. It's all right for men to have their own mode of grief, but if they hide their feelings away in a box and just rail and get angry, they may end up with substance addictions, experience physical ailments, and sink into depression more easily.

On the other hand, women are intuitive grievers. They intuitively express their emotions openly, finding other women to listen to them and sympathize. Women often are the ones with lots of what-if and if-only questions. They feel more guilt about their loss and cogitate over the story, trying to figure out how they could have done better. But women also have an easy command of the language to help them through both their guilt and their grief.

If you want to help a man in grief, be aware of the following.

➡ Men feel loss the same way; they just can't express it.

➡ A man has physical differences that can affect his grieving process.

➡ A man's grief may be more future-centric than a woman's.

➡ Men need to find active ways to express their grief.

➡ Just because a man is quiet, doesn't mean he isn't in grief.

➡ Men prefer more alone time to ponder their grief.

➡ Ask a man "How are you doing today?" instead of "How are you feeling today?" Men can't verbalize as easily as women can.

➡ Encourage men to tell their stories by prompting them, "Please tell me how it happened."

➡ Despite cultural platitudes, men need to be encouraged to process their grief openly.

HOW LONG WILL MY GRIEF LAST?

Kronos Time vs. Kairos Time

THE ANCIENT GREEKS HAD two words for time. The first was Kronos (as in the English words "chronological" or "anachronism"). We know Kronos as clock time—time that is measurable by seconds, minutes, hours, or years. Kronos time is linear, sequential time, gauged by a calendar, and it describes the breadth of the past, present, and future. Kronos time is on a tight leash, moving inexorably out of the past toward a fixed future, with a dearth of freedom or movement. Kronos time is full of deadlines, schedules, agendas, and annoying beeps. In Kronos time, you measure moments, making it totally quantitative time.

Kairos time is qualitative. If you are counting Kairos time, you are in carpe diem mode, where you seize the day, hour, or fleeting second. Kairos time is capturing the right moment, the opportune time, the perfect minute. Kairos time signifies a time lapse, a moment of indeterminate time in which things transpire. Kairos is spiritual time that is creative and full of serendipity. It is the time of fantasies, and it cannot be restrained. Kairos is globular, oscillating back and forth, without the constraints of limiting boundaries. Kairos time slows life down, whereas Kronos time is all about speed.

The Greeks personified Kronos (a.k.a. Saturn, to the Romans) as an old Father Time type of character, hunched over with a long gray beard, carrying a scythe and an hourglass. I picture him as a very aged Michael Gambon in Harry Potter. On the other hand, Kairos (a.k.a. Caerus, to the Romans) was personified as a great-looking youth, with a lock of hair hanging across his forehead. He represents the expedient, or opportune, occasion, since opportunity never gets old and beauty is always applauded. He stands on his tiptoes because he is always running, and he has wings on his feet to fly with the wind. I think of him as a cool Liam Hemsworth or Taylor Lautner kind of guy. OK, I really see a young Cary Grant, but that ages me to the max. Was anyone ever as cool as Cary Grant?

When Peter died, I was mired in Kronos time. I measured my time in seconds. I couldn't fathom how I would get through the next minute, let alone make it through the day. I stared at the clock, pleading for sleep to alleviate my pain. I tried to keep busy to ward off the shock and pain. I was in a Kronos mind-set, and it took time to change my outlook.

After almost a year and a half, I am beginning to immerse myself in Kairos time. I am open to capturing new memories and cherish the fleetingness of life. I am cataloging these good moments to put in my new treasured album of recollections. I am trying to keep Kairos time, by giving each moment a purpose. I am trying to savor and value each moment, and stop running long enough to enjoy the view. How long will this take? My Kairos gauge says it will take as long as I need, and I'm OK with that.

CONTINUING BONDS
(No, Not Municipal Bonds!)

GRIEF IS STILL A four-letter word in my vocabulary (yes, yes, it is five but who's counting), and one that often rhymes with muck, but I have learned to use grief in a positive way to plow forward on my journey towards a modicum of restoration in my life. I have learned that there is no "normal" way to grieve. Grievers are like snowflakes. There are definitely no two alike. Each of us grieves in our own manner, in our own style, and at our own pace.

Up until the middle of the last century, the thinking among grief therapists and psychologists was that the bereaved emotionally detach themselves from the deceased. Sigmund Freud devoutly espoused this theory because he believed that the mourner should be freed from his attachments in order to move ahead and form new relationships. The psychiatrist John Bowlby totally differed from Freud. Bowlby felt that talking about the dead without finding room for the deceased in one's self, would be like Hamlet without the Prince. In 1966 Dennis Klass, Phyllis Silverman, and Steven Nickman helped to change this current theory with their book *Continuing Bonds: New Understands of Grief.* This book changed the current method of grief therapy, citing many cases where continuing bonds provided comfort and support in coping with grief.

I have learned that grief does not end. It is an ongoing process in which Peter and I figure out how we will go on together. Yes, Peter's connection and bond are within my heart and soul. He is still my go-to support system. When I need him, I can talk to him, breathe with him, or just conjure up an image which will help me through the tough times. In life, he was my moral compass. In death he performs that role as well, bequeathing me the wisdom to forge forward. You might think that I am living in the past. On the contrary, I am living in the present with Peter guiding me through this maze of grief.

Here are a few ways you can form continuing bonds with your late loved one:

➡ Talk to your lost love. I know this sounds crazy but it works big time. I talk to Peter all the time and I feel comforted just knowing he is surrounding me in spirit. Avoid doing this in public unless you are wearing headphones, in which case everyone will assume you are on a phone call and won't care!

➡ Write a letter to your loved one. You will find that you can pour out your heart openly and it is totally cathartic. Not great on the mascara, but it is a wonderful release and connection all at once.

➡ Talk about your loved one with friends and family. Tell stories to new friends and you will feel the love.

➡ Perform a ritual like lighting a candle to keep your loved one in your memory and your heart.

➡ On special occasions or holidays, make a toast to your loved one. Out family leaves a door open for Elijah at Passover. I leave a chair next to me to remember Peter. Besides, I get to eat a double portion of matzo ball soup!

➡ Plant a tree in his or her memory and watch it grow.

➡ Wear your loved one's wedding ring on another hand. I have linked all the rings we had together on a chain which sits over my heart and provides constant comfort.

➡ Prepare your loved one's favorite dishes. This is not great for my health because Peter loved meat, potatoes, and butter. But occasionally I will splurge and have a steak and fries and revel in the comfort food, and the comfort it affords me.

➡ Finish a project that your loved one started. Patton Oswalt finished his deceased wife's book which helped him in his process. I was thinking of taking up golf in Peter's memory but neither of us would have been happy with that choice! I still believe that golf is "a good walk spoiled."

➡ Know that your loved one would be proud of you. He or she would understand that you have to plow through the process of grief. But they would also want you to live a life worthy of the two of you. I honor Peter by allowing him to guide me on my journey as my partner and soulmate.

EXIT LAUGHING
Comic Relief

It is bad to suppress laughter.
It goes back down and spreads to your hips.
—FRED ALLEN

IT IS A GIVEN that laughter is the best medicine. When we laugh, we feel a spark of happiness. Not only do we feel better in our guffawing, but research has shown that laughter strengthens our immune system, improves our concentration levels, ups our endorphin levels, lowers our blood pressure, and increases the production of T-cells, which help the pituitary gland to release its own pain-suppressing opiates. Sounds like a plus all around, right? Ever since 1981, when Norman Cousins talked of overcoming a fatal disease by watching Charlie Chaplin movies, in his book *Anatomy of an Illness,* scientists have been taking a serious look at laughter.

In Japan, laughter clubs have sprung up all over, and there is even an international laughter championship to determine Japan's best laugher. Laughter yoga is also on the rise. Laughter has the power to work the stomach, chest, neck, and facial muscles. The clubs meet in public parks, and the sessions are totally free, with voluntary donations. Advocates of this laughter movement laugh off skeptics, noting the increase in their levels of happiness. Sorry for the puns, but I just can't help myself. Ha-ha.

Since Peter died I have used humor in my writing and throughout my daily life to help me through grief. I have no guilt about cracking a joke in my grief group. I have no qualms about laughing out loud to get me through this arduous journey of grief. Viktor Frankl in *Man's Search for Meaning* said, "I never would have made it if I could not have laughed. It lifted me momentarily out of this horrible situation, just enough to make it livable." Sigmund Freud argued that laughter is a coping mechanism for dealing with the unspeakable pains of life. Laughter isn't just about comedy. Behind every joke is a temporary tragedy. Who doesn't laugh uproariously, when he or she sees a man slip on a banana peel and fall?

Peter loved fart jokes. If he was sad, he would watch the bean-eating campfire scene in *Blazing Saddles*, and he'd feel better. Other cheer-up movie lines for us included "There's no reason to become alarmed, and we hope you'll enjoy the rest of your flight. By the way, is there anyone on board who knows how to fly a plane?" from *Airplane*; "Nice beaver" and "Thank you. I just had it stuffed," from *The Naked Gun: From the Files of Police Squad!*; "'Let's do what one shepherd said to the other shepherd.' 'What?' 'Let's get the flock outta here,'" from *Lethal Weapon*; "Are you crying? There's no crying! There's no crying in baseball!" from *A League of Their Own*; "Thank you very little," from *Caddyshack*; and, of course, "I'll have what she's having," from *When Harry Met Sally*.

According to Wikipedia, "gallows humor" is defined as "witticism in the face of—and in response to—a hopeless situation. It arises from stressful, traumatic, or life-threatening situations, often in circumstances such that death is perceived as impending and unavoidable." Gallows humor is a tool used to diffuse a stressful situation. The following joke is an example of gallows humor. It is dark and weird, yet it made me laugh:

> A couple of hunters are out in the woods when one of them falls to the ground. He doesn't seem to be breathing, and his eyes are rolled back into his head. The other guy whips out his cell phone and calls the emergency services. He gasps to the operator, "My friend is dead! What can I do?" The operator, in a calm, soothing voice, says, "Just take it easy. I can help. First, let's make sure he's dead." There is a silence; then a loud gunshot is heard. The guy's voice comes back on the line. He says, "OK, now what?"

I know that Peter would not want me to be miserable in my grief. He would be the first person to tell me to laugh as a path toward healing. Laughter is an important tool to use. So, for Peter, I will continue to live by the motto "he who laughs, lasts!"

LAURIE'S FUNNY PLAN OF ACTION

➡ Watch as many Mel Brooks movies as possible.

➡ Listen to Billy Crystal's autobiography, *Still Foolin' 'Em: Where I'm Going; and Where the Hell Are My Keys?* Or Martin Short's *I Must Say: My Life as a Humble Comedy Legend*.

➡ Watch *Funny British Animal Voiceovers* on YouTube.

➡ Marathon binge-watch *Will & Grace*, *Friends*, and *The Big Bang Theory*.

➡ Look at old photos of myself in high school and laugh at my pathetic hairdo.

➡ Ask Siri or Alexa to tell me a joke. It will be a groaner!

➡ Paint my toenails a weird color.

➡ Watch this video of a baby laughing at ripped paper! This never fails to up my mood! **wimp.com/ baby-laughing-hysterically-at-ripping-paper**

LONELINESS VERSUS SOLITUDE

MANY WRONGLY ASSUME THAT solitude and loneliness are the same state of being. Both are characterized by solitariness, but the resemblance ends there. Loneliness in grief is a form of isolation where one feels that something is missing. Loneliness is not a choice. When Peter died, I was thrust into loneliness. Loneliness is a negative state of discontent, marked by estrangement and aloneness. I felt excluded, unwanted, unimportant, and my self-esteem hit rock bottom. I considered loneliness a very harsh punishment, a state of deficiency, a state of estrangement, and an unwelcome awareness of my aloneness. Even when I was surrounded by loved ones, I still experienced loneliness. Loneliness sucks!

Solitude, on the other hand, is the state of being alone without being lonely. Solitude is a beneficial and constructive choice. After Peter died, and still to this day, I often choose the quiet of solitude to work through my grief. Solitude helps me read books on grief and digest the material. Solitude gives me the time to organize my thoughts into essays that help in my process. Solitude has become my sixth sense for finding a path to restoration. Solitude is a positive time for inner reflection. In solitude, I have found sufficient company. In solitude, I have learned to cherish myself.

After Peter died, I was so lonely that I couldn't bear the silence. I turned to Amazon Echo for music (mostly the music from *Hamilton*); I turned on the television for background noise; and I reached out to friends for comfort. The suddenness of my loneliness brought back childhood memories of abandonment. I felt like the little girl waiting for my mother to come home to make me a complete person. The loneliness catapulted me back to unhappier times when I felt unloved. Peter was my good parent, my lover, and my other half. Now I had to look to the little girl inside and make her feel loved again. I had to transform my intense feelings of loss and loneliness into comfort for that sad part of me. I had to make friends with my inner self. In my solitude of reflection, I had to find a person inside me with whom I could enjoy just hanging out. I had to find my best friend within this lanky body I call home.

Transforming loneliness into solitude isn't easy. I began by talking to myself a lot. I'm not talking about the conversation you have while screaming at your computer. I am talking about asking yourself, "Is it dinnertime yet?" I found myself talking to the characters on television shows. I found myself commenting on a great fried egg on toast I was eating. I had to find a friend in me. I had to draw sustenance from the quiet. I had to regain a perspective on my life in order to restore my soul.

The loneliness of grief is devastating. Life is about relationships, and we are all social creatures who don't classically deal well with the pain of loss. It requires a huge amount of time and effort to power through. You have lost pieces of your heart, and you must rebuild yourself. Once you have accepted that you will never fill the void of your loss, you can start finding a love for your inner self to help you adapt to your new life as a singular person.

I recently formulated a list of suggestions for coping with loneliness and opening oneself up to the goodness of solitude:

➡ Reach out to friends and family who give you solace. They are the ones who don't dispense with platitudes and who diligently listen to your story of woe without any judgments. Our passage through grief may be lonely, but we do *not* have to journey alone.

➡ Don't expect others to guess what you need. Tell them point-blank if you need a hug, or a ride, or just an ear.

➡ Be honest about everything. If you need some alone time, ask for it. If you need your light bulb replaced, ask for that.

➡ Have a good cry. Let it all hang out.

➡ Find some good solitude time to remember your loved one and then cry again.

➡ Don't lash out at others in your pain. Be mindful that they don't know what to say to you.

➡ Join a support group. Those in your support group are the only ones who will really get your pain.

➡ Identify your loneliest times and see if you can alter your routine. My worst times are the weekends, so I make plans well in advance to ensure I am not alone for too long.

➡ Make a comforting meal. Cooking can be therapeutic.

➡ Make daily to-do lists. The routine will help you move forward. By all means, add a little retail therapy if that helps!

➡ Journalize. Writing is empowering as a tool for discovering your true feelings.

➡ Take walks or work out. The endorphins work wonders.

➡ Embrace solitude. It can be an adventure. Use the time to reflect, remember, or just be happy with you, yourself, and the new you!

Language has created the word "loneliness"
to express the pain of being alone. And it has created the
word "solitude" to express the glory of being alone.
—PAUL TILLICH

SELF-COMPASSION
The Key to Getting through Grief

*Remember, you have been criticizing yourself for years and it
hasn't worked. Try approving of yourself and see what happens.*
—LOUISE L. HAY

GRIEF IS THE PROCESS of acceptance. Acceptance happens when we
let go of expectations. Expectations lead to resentment, which keeps us
stuck in self-criticism. Self-criticism keeps us mired in the pain of grief.
It is a cycle that hits us most when we are in the depths of despair.

When my incredible husband Peter died, I was drowning in an
ocean of pain. I couldn't catch my breath under the sea of sorrow I was
experiencing. I couldn't find my way to the top to breathe again. Even
though I was surrounded by family and friends, I felt alienated. I was
alone for the first time in my life, and the feelings of abandonment and
loneliness overwhelmed me. I needed to unmask my self-compassion
to help me through my journey.

Compassion is a desire to help others who are suffering. Tenderness,
kindness, sympathy, and understanding define compassion. I was pretty good at being compassionate to others, but I found that I could not
find the strength to be compassionate to myself. I was critical of my
process. I found myself saying, "I am not getting better fast enough,"
or "I should be out and about by now." To keep me going, I had to
dangle the carrot of remembering that I was once happy. I had to find
the fortitude to believe I might be happy again. I had to visualize a

pleasurable time ahead. I had to realize that I hadn't lost control of my life. I had to understand that I had a choice to make. I alone could decide how grief was going to affect the rest of my life. I had to find the strength to believe that when confronted with loss, I could survive.

Practicing self-compassion allows me to see that grief is the other side of the coin of love. I have loved deeply, and now I am grieving that loss. Therefore, I must somehow, and this is the tricky part, learn to accept the loss and pain and be mindful of my process. I have to be careful to pace myself and not process all the pain at once. I have to be good to myself and take breaks by watching drop-dead (OK, forgive the pun) funny movies like *Blazing Saddles* and eating creamy tomato soup and grilled cheese sandwiches. Yes, I have to bring out the compassion in me, and shelve the critical Laurie who doesn't allow for imperfection. I have to accept the understanding that I will have a tough road, and the only path ahead needs to be strewn with the roses of compassion. I would never be harsh to a friend in pain, so I must remember to reverse the golden rule and "do unto myself as I would do unto others."

Self-esteem is all about being special, better than others. Self-compassion is all about being ordinary and sharing in others' pain. Self-compassion is about being human, and frail, and accepting of all that it entails. When Peter and I had an argument, which wasn't very often, one of us would quickly say, "Mea culpa, it's my fault." We used to laugh at Jack Palance in *City Slickers*, when he held up one finger, meaning the "one thing" that would indicate the meaning of life. Our "one thing" was admitting that neither of us had to be right. Believe me, that is no easy concept to pull off! Practicing forgiveness was hard to do on a regular basis, but it was why our marriage worked for so many years.

The knowledge that I am not alone in my suffering is immensely helpful. At first I looked in the mirror and saw the substantial sadness in my face. I felt isolated and was pissed off that others had perfect lives while mine was defective and imperfect. But seeing my support-group members in the same pain helped me to feel more connected with them and with life.

Part of learning self-compassion made me imagine myself as a skilled physician who would show me a soothing and gentle bedside manner. Hard to imagine these days, right? I had to train myself to embrace my spirit of survival.

The following tips will help you find a bit more self-compassion in your life:

- ➡ Speak to yourself à la Mark Darcy in *Bridget Jones's Diary*: "I like you, very much. Just as you are."

- ➡ Treat yourself to retail therapy, lots of dark chocolate, or a massage!

- ➡ Make a list of all the good qualities you have and recite them as a mantra, but only to yourself!

- ➡ Try to make a list of what gifts of gratitude you have in your life, be it kids, grandkids, friends, or just a good haircut! Recent research indicates that being grateful is a mood booster.

- ➡ Treat yourself as you would your best buddy!

- ➡ Breathe! Get more oxygen to your brain by taking slow, deep, and calming breaths.

- ➡ Try thinking about how you have survived other tough times and will continue to survive grief.

- ➡ Instead of beating yourself up for not doing well, try using an imaginary Reset button and believe you can persevere through it.

- ➡ Write your feelings down in a journal.

- ➡ Keep your expectations of yourself and others realistic. Be flexible. Ask how much it really matters, and do only what is within your capabilities.

- ➡ Step back, use perspective, and applaud your progress, and that means even the small steps.

➡ Don't sweat the small stuff! After what you have endured, the small stuff seems like meaningless crap!

➡ Say no to things you do not want to do! *When I Say No, I Feel Guilty* is a book that tells volumes about this subject. This is the year of no. Hell, it's the decade of no!

➡ If you want a break, take a break!

➡ Just because you feel bad, doesn't mean you are bad! Stop blaming yourself.

➡ Cry if you need. Watch the show *This Is Us* and sob. It's cathartic.

➡ Be compassionate with others, which will build up your self-esteem.

➡ Remove toxic friends from your life!

➡ Try to commit to a daily mantra of "My name is… and I really love you."

EMPATHY VERSUS SYMPATHY

If you're looking for sympathy you'll find it between
shit and syphilis in the dictionary.
—DAVID SEDARIS

THE TERMS "EMPATHY" AND "sympathy" are often used inter-changeably, but they have quite different meanings, and varied and veiled connotations. The differences between the terms are attributed to emotional factors rather than grammar. Both empathy and sympathy are forms of concern for another person's well-being. The easiest way to describe empathy is the act of putting yourself in someone else's shoes. Empathy occurs when you are truly trying to understand or experience someone else's emotions, as if they were your own. Empathy is a shared experience. Sympathy is saying what is expected, often laced with platitudes. In today's current parlance, sympathy has a negative-tinged characteristic that almost comes out as pity. It is natural to want to make things better for others, but it doesn't always work that way. On the other hand, when you are empathetic, you do your own golden rule and "treat others as you would like to be treated."

Both sympathy and empathy have roots in the Greek term "pathos," meaning suffering and feeling. Empathy is formed from the ancient Greek work "empatheia" with the prefix "en" plus the root "pathos," meaning feeling, which literally means "in feeling." Sympathy is from the Greek word "sympatheia" and is formed from the prefix "sum," meaning together, combined with "pathos," which translates to mean "together feeling or together suffering." Sympathy is the older of the two terms, dating back to the mid-1500s. Sympathy is more of an act of commiseration and an acknowledgment of another's grief. But sympathy often has pejorative connotations, with thoughts of lacy greeting cards and corny prosaicisms.

Empathy is the newer of the two words and first appeared in English in 1909, when it was translated by Edward Bradford Titchener from the German "Einfühlung," an old concept that had been gaining new meaning and increased relevance from the 1870s onward. Empathy, at the turn of the century, was used to describe a unique combination of intellectual effort and bodily feelings, thought to characterize visual experiences.

Now that I have dumped all over the term "sympathy," it still has a place in our lexicon. Sympathy is a virtue; it's just that empathy wins out in a head-to-head contest, particularly when you are dealing with someone in grief. Research has shown that you can boost your empathy levels by doing certain things like reading more fiction and thus immersing yourself in the characters' lives. I would also argue that watching a tearjerker, four-hankie movie can improve your empathy skills. Besides, a good cry never hurt anyone. Being in tune with others is great, but it does require Costco-sized boxes of tissues. I also think that empathy skills, like self-compassion, can be internalized. Just listening more, sharing in other people's joy, and learning to read facial expressions might give you the tools to become more empathetic.

If you really want to test out your empathy level, try this online test to help you better understand where you stand in the empathic arena: **greatergood.berkeley.edu/quizzes/take_quiz/14**.

Feel free to contact me with the results at my website, **lauriegrad.com**.

~~~~~~

THE OPTIMISM BIAS
It Won't Happen to Me

A pessimist sees the difficulty in every opportunity;
an optimist sees the opportunity in every difficulty.
—WINSTON S. CHURCHILL

THE OPTIMISM BIAS IS the belief that each of us is more likely to experience positive outcomes and less likely to have negative ones befall us. It is the belief that the future will be more improved than the past. We see this optimism in kids fantasizing about growing up. Most adults envision the optimism bias as a glass more than half full.

I think of the optimism bias more as a self-protective touch of positive narcissism. It is good to imagine we are smart, healthy, popular, and attractive. This is the optimism bias with an encouraging tweak. It is wonderful to sail through life imagining lovely things. The downside of the optimism bias is that we disregard the reality of an overall situation because we think we are excluded from the merciless nightmares of life. The optimism bias, at its worst, is when we tend to disregard warning labels in life and falsely assume we are invincible. Many continue to smoke cigarettes, despite the warnings of health problems. Many drive while drunk despite the information that tells us it invariably leads to accidents or even death. On the other hand, the optimism bias helps one focus on the positive, and research has shown that an upbeat outlook can physically help our bodies to fight stress and disease. The optimism bias keeps us moving forward and fighting for our best existence.

I used this form of mental time travel until Peter died. I perpetually moved back and forth through time and space in my mind, thinking of all the good things in our future. Then the unthinkable happened. Peter died, and I couldn't believe that it had happened to me. I had clearly underestimated the odds of personal misfortune and overestimated the view through my rose-colored glasses. I was playing Cleopatra, "the Queen of De-Nile." I was patently hard-wired for hope, and now I was shocked that my world was crumbling with the loss of my love. Sure, I had thought about the possibility of Peter's death, but I had quickly rewired my brain into an obliviousness of positivity. Perhaps if I had stuck with Susan Sontag's "If I expect as little as possible, I won't be hurt"? But no one can prepare you for grief and its ramifications. No one can tell you about this journey you will travel. No amount of optimism can stave off the pain of grief. I just couldn't believe that this was happening to me. I'd had the illusion that I was in control of my life, but the inevitable happened, and now I had to play out my grief.

I decided to study optimism as a tool. I looked up the definition and got "a disposition or tendency to look on the more favorable side of events or conditions and to expect the most favorable outcome." Before Peter died I used rationalization to achieve optimism. It wasn't magical thinking, but I did put on blinders when we visited doctors, ignoring the bad stuff and convincing us both that all would be OK. We adapted to the news and soldiered on, living fully to the max. I garnered strength from optimism. I discovered an inner belief in myself that knew I had the power to be strong.

I now use the optimism bias to my advantage. A little delusional thinking is not so bad, on occasion. I have decided to use AAA as my mantra. No, not the auto club (although it is a mighty fine organization), but an acronym I have devised to move ahead:

➡ I will Acknowledge the reality of Peter's death.

➡ I will Accept the certainty of the loss.

➡ I will Act positively as a means to move forward toward my new normal.

➡ I will also use optimism as an Asset to my Advantage. (Why not throw in a few more As?)

➡ I am trying to fill my glass, milliliter by milliliter, using Audacity and optimism, as well as the support of friends and family, to once again focus on the plusses in my life's path.

SHIFTING THE ASSUMPTIVE WORLD VIEW
Putting Your Shattered World Back Together

Never assume because when you assume it
makes an ass *out of* u *and* me.
—FELIX UNGER IN NEIL SIMON'S *THE ODD COUPLE*

THE OPTIMISM BIAS IS the belief that each of us is more likely to experience positive outcomes and less likely to have negative ones transpire. In order to get us through life, we live in an assumptive world, where our assumptions or beliefs that ground and secure us, will be not be disturbed.

Death and other forms of loss are complete shocks to our assumptive world. Trauma devastates our assumptive world, and we are shaken to the core, making us full of shame and insecurity. The process of grief causes us to come to terms with the annihilation of our assumptive world and its belief system. We must heal and transform what was once our assumptive world into a new world order. We must rebuild the foundation of our belief system and begin to trust ourselves, others, and the world's crises, in order to move forward. Our spirituality has been traumatized beyond measure, and what was once a safe and protected world is now in shambles and must be restructured.

The loss of our loved one throws us into secondary losses as well. Not only have we lost our compass, our tiller, and our cheerleader, but we have lost social standing, financial security, and companionship. We had a treasure map for the future, and now that map goes nowhere, and the treasure eludes us. We have to reexamine all the assumptions we lived by in the past, and find a way to rebuild the house of our being. The trauma of loss has shaken our foundations, and we have to find the mortar and bricks, and the little pigs to come build it, not of straw, but of solid material that will make us stand tall again.

Peter died suddenly in front of my very eyes. The trauma of that experience was a betrayal of my assumptive world. How could this have happened? My assumptive world was my attachment to Peter and all this entailed. Now I have lost that assumptive world, and I am trying to build it again, pillar by pillar. I have to make sure that each piece of material that I use to rebuild my life is securely set in place. No termites allowed in this rebuilding, please! I am utilizing the trust of my family and friendships as a basic material for my new life. I have to find a new personal definition of Laurie alone. But I will never lose the love of Peter, which is part of my foundation. He is attached in my heart even though he is not physically present. Peter made me a better person, and I am using his image as a medium to build myself back into a new assumptive world, one where I will venture forth gingerly but with a modicum of hope. My assumptive world was shattered, giving way to profound grief and emotion. But little by little, brick by brick, friend by friend, and mini-joy by mini-joy, those emotions have energized me toward a healing path.

Your assumptions are your windows on the world.
Scrub them off every once in a while, or the light won't come in.
—ISAAC ASIMOV

DON'T POSTPONE JOY
Smell the Damn Roses!

You live but once, you might as well be amusing.
—COCO CHANEL

BPD (BEFORE PETER DIED), I took so much of life for granted. It is true that Peter and I lived life fully, enjoying each other and loving life, but we were often too busy to take pleasure in our activities and make them more valuable. We didn't take the precious time to tuck them away as cherished memories. Even though we were living life to the fullest, we still postponed joy. Peter never got to fulfill his bucket list. There were more trips we should have taken together; more adventures to pursue; more missed opportunities; and more times when we should have basked in our oneness.

Death is a great teacher, but often too late. Once I lost Peter, I had to discover what lay beneath the surface of my soul. I was no longer part of a couple. I had to sift through the wreckage of grief to discover the depth of my being and to unearth who I truly was on my own. In the face of profound loss, what I knew to be myself was trashed. I had to find my authentic self in the vestiges of my being. I had to follow the Shakespearean tenant "to thine own self be true." I had to peel away the layers of my persona like an artichoke, to get to the heart and most appetizing part of me. I had to turn on the inner light inside me and do what made me happy, truly happy.

I accomplished this task step by step. When invited to something

I didn't want to do, I began to say no, with gusto. Maybe not gusto—I still have some modicum of tact—but I did take care of myself and say no, honoring my genuine wishes. Man, does that feel good! Don't want to go to a party? Say no. Don't want to talk to someone who makes you miserable? Allow it to go to voice mail. Are you following so far? In simple terms, I was being honest with myself and taking care of Laurie to the max, which ultimately made me smile and ergo brought me some joy! I finally could honor the needs inside me and find in my inner self the truth that needed to be validated. For the first time since Peter died, I was living authentically, safeguarding my beliefs, my values, and most importantly, my desires, or lack thereof. I had a new protective navigation system in my head to guide me, protect me, and care for my needs. I was finding my own empowerment, which had been decimated by grief.

APD (after Peter died), I learned that life is only in the here and now. I can't wallow in the past or look to the future. Both the past and the future are too scary for me at this moment in my journey. I must exclusively focus on keeping the present in my sight line. I have also learned how to savor each step of life. I have never been a particularly patient person. I tend to eat too fast and move too fast, which often makes for bruised shins, ouch! "Hurry" has always been my middle name. But hurrying is not sage and good counsel. I remember the parable of the tortoise and the hare. Slow and steady wins the race!

According to astronomers, after a star has died, its light continues to glow for millions of years. Peter's light is radiating within me, within my son, within my grandchildren, and within all who were touched by him. Knowing that helps me to not postpone joy. I am on a quest to rediscover pleasure. I must focus on the good times and savor them. I have to put the g back in gratitude and understand how to forgive others and myself. I have to smell the damn roses, without sneezing! Life is like an ice cream cone. Lick the hell out of it before it melts!

Some people feel the rain. Others just get wet.
—ROGER MILLER

~~~~~~

FLYING SOLO

Traveling Alone Sucks!

Those who fly solo have the strongest wings.
—UNKNOWN

EVERY TIME PETER AND I traveled together, we would settle into our seats on the airplane. As the plane took off, he would lace my much-smaller fingers cozily into his sizable digits. As the plane climbed upward, we would grip each other's hand, sometimes tighter than blood flow allowed, especially if the level of bumpiness was off the charts! We always continued to clutch hands until the plane safely reached its altitude. As we got older, we amended the pattern to holding each other's hands just until we leveled off, saving on circulation woes. This comforting tradition made each of us feel safe and secure with the stress of flying.

The tradition started on our honeymoon. We had just been married in a small ceremony of twelve people. Peter was dressed in his finest preppy gray suit, wearing a white boutonnière of freesia, my favorite flower. I, on the other hand, was wearing a white brocade miniskirt and Courrèges boots, with some ridiculous pillbox hat that made me look like a cross between the model Twiggy and a bellhop. Even though it was the sixties, what was I thinking? Note, said pic included. *Insert laughter here!*

We had only known each other four months. We met on October 17, 1967, got engaged on December 21, and were married on February 11. We both were aware that cupid had struck us big time with a soul mate's

arrow. We were instantly best friends, and it turned out it was dumb luck that we had found each other by a fluke encounter.

After a very brief wedding, where the rabbi shook more than either of us, concluding with a repulsively raw beef Wellington, we flew to Nassau's Paradise Island. Huntington Hartford had just opened what was purported to be the most luxurious hotel, called the Ocean Club. Our honeymoon suite, however, turned out to be two twin beds racked together sideways with a lump in the middle. So much for luxury. On the flight down, we began the hand clutch that would be our takeoff and landing tradition for forty-seven years. On some occasions, we even clutched hands across the aisles as the flight attendants scowled at us.

Since Peter died, I have been literally and figuratively flying solo. The synonyms for "solo" are "alone" and "solitary" (so sad), "unaccompanied" (sounds like I need a tag to fly as a minor), "unescorted" (hoping for an escort soon), "unattended" (but I am attended by so many friends and family), "unchaperoned" (not a chance of a chaperone at this age), "unaided" (does early boarding count?), and my favorite, "independent," which gives me the hope that I am growing. In the more than two years since Peter died, I have learned, from the many blogs I have written, and the countless hours of grief I have slogged through, that I have found the strength to do solo pretty well. I have found the power to love me, myself, and I, and take her with me as I fly commercial airlines, or as I fly emotionally on my way to finding my new acceptably different, and hopefully positive, future existence.

THE POWER OF THE KEYBOARD
Writing My Way through Grief

I can shake off everything as I write;
my sorrows disappear, my courage is reborn.
—ANNE FRANK

OUR WESTERN VALUES ARE not culturally equipped for grief. Death is such a taboo that we call it the "d-word," the way we used to refer to cancer as the "c-word." When we tag grief as a taboo, it becomes a dreadful surprise and shock, and we are not primed to deal with its ramifications. When Peter died, I was in total disbelief. How could this befall me? How could he suddenly be gone from my life?

After my tragic loss, the one thing that saved me was writing. When I was little, I would write funny poetry à la Ogden Nash. I would compose hilarious stories with weird and wacky characters. I loved writing, but when I became a food writer, recipes were my outlet. When I was suddenly thrust into widowhood, I returned to writing prose, and it became a much-needed release from the immense feelings of pain that clouded my horizons. When I was little, a new notebook and pens brought a smile to my face. I treasured my paper and pens as if they were jewels. Now, my keyboard is my savior. I can type away for hours, get my feelings into the computer, and feel a whole lot better about my existence. I can pull all the threads of my ideas into a concept to be woven into an essay. I type away in stream-of-consciousness style, and keep writing until I achieve a sense of peace or at least a grammatically cohesive bunch of sentences, with enough humor to keep me smiling.

Writing is one of the oldest methods of expressiveness. People diarize or journalize constantly to relieve stress. I never did that until I was faced with grief. Now I write with a need to release the pressure of grief that builds up in my soul. The writing helps me clarify the confusion and conflicting emotions that surface daily. With my keyboard, I can reflect on the meaning of Peter's death. Once I have put my thoughts and feelings into the computer, I can sit back and relax. I know they are there, and they will be there so I can review them and perceive the progress I have made as I trek through the valley of grief.

Journalizing in grief is a powerful tool. Many people set up a regular time to write. Those with artistic talent have the ability to draw their feelings on paper. My drawing skills are limited to doodling pictures of Charlie Brown and Snoopy, so I channel prose as my conduit. The key for me is to write when I am motivated. By using the computer, I maintain a record of the dates, and I can therefore look at my progress and feel pride in the small steps I have made toward restoration. I sometimes record dreams or write letters to Peter, and a few letters to grief, letting him know that I am not pleased that I have to deal with him on a daily basis!

If you are having trouble journaling, try these thought triggers to start you off:

➤ Today I…

➤ I was really infuriated today when…

➤ I fell apart today because…

➤ I finally did it. I succeeded at…

➤ Today was a killer…

➤ Tomorrow, I will try to…

➤ I know I'm getting better because…

Writing is my way to make sense of what has happened in my life. When I started to blog, I was embarrassed by my extreme sorrow. I was ill prepared for the power of death and used writing to find my way. I was so baffled by my grief that I had to pour my words onto the paper to make the unspeakable fathomable. In the depth of grief's grip, the only release I had was writing. Profound loss leaves us flailing, unable to comprehend our loss. Speaking my pain, and blogging about it weekly, has returned my vocal powers. Knowing that I am giving voice to the d-word and the g-word has helped me, and other widows and widowers who follow my blogs, cope with the art of living again.

My name is Laurie, and I am a proud writer.

A NEW CHAPTER

WTF, IS THIS THE NEW NORMAL?

WE THINK OF THE word "normal" as conforming to a standard or pattern. Normal is what is expected—SOP (standard operating procedure). "The new normal" is defined as "a previously unfamiliar or atypical situation that has become standard, usual, or expected." Once you have experienced the profound loss of a loved one, you are forever changed. Peter's sudden and unexpected death shredded my heart, and I knew that my life would never be the same. What was once "normal" in my day-to-day existence now seemed totally unfathomable. I wanted desperately to press the Reset button and find something that at least circled the neighborhood of the word "acceptable"! Normal forever died with Peter.

The only normal I could muster up was abnormal, which totally made me laugh, thinking of the funny scene in *Young Frankenstein* with Gene Wilder and Marty Feldman. After dropping a genius brain jar for Frederick Frankenstein to implant in his creature, Igor (pronounced eye-gore) picks up an "abnormal" brain. The monster awakes and nearly kills Frankenstein. When questioned, Igor confesses he'd dropped the first brain and picked up someone else's, "Abby...someone. Abby Normal."

We are often so intently busy doing our life chores that we don't take the time to look at the bigger picture. When we are faced with a catastrophic or traumatic event such as a death or a messy divorce, it is almost too late to regroup. The world keeps spinning round and round at a fever pitch, and we don't have time to take the necessary emotional and cerebral deep breaths to get us through the grieving process. We want to press the Pause button *stat*, in order to stop the

259

world spinning long enough to relocate our lost equilibrium. Western society doesn't allow us to take the time to work through immense loss and come out the other side. Women, particularly, are hard-wired to be damage-control experts, especially capable of helping others, not necessarily ourselves. But when traumas like the death of a spouse occur, we crumble (to quote Mel Brooks yet again) "like a bunch of broccoli." Women are the movers and shakers, and now as widows, we have been broken to the core.

Many people assume that getting used to the new normal implies that you are a damaged person and you must accept the defacement of your soul. Quite the opposite is true. Grief restoration enables you to fully experience what life has to offer, including a new relationship and joy experienced to the max. I will forever miss Peter and our life together. But I have set a goal for my new normal: to try to forget the bad memories and only pluck out the good ones that will hopefully bring a smile to my face one day soon.

This is when finding a new normal becomes a full-on positive choice. This is when we choose to call in the cavalry of friends, family, and counselors, along with vats of chocolate ice cream, as tools to get us through our broken phase, and heal the parts of us enough, that we can learn to walk again, in what will be a new form of normalcy. We are eternally changed and forever broken. Loss takes away the validation of our identity. Trauma and pain bring grief, which allows us to shift and pass forward through time, transforming us through this never-ending love story, and allowing us to see fresh perspectives of a newly formed temporal existence. An astronaut will tell you that the biggest challenge on a space flight is reentry. Reentry after the loss of a spouse is a monumental adjustment. Your life has been turned upside down, and you have to adjust to being solo after having been part of a close-knit couple. You will never find normal again, but you will adapt little by little to cooking, eating, sleeping, walking, and breathing alone.

Normalcy, even a new kind of normalcy, does not jibe well in my reckoning with grief. A new chapter is a possibility, or I might be able to identify my life as different. "Acceptably different" seems a whole lot better than "a new normal." With "different," I am more fluid and flexible to choose my own dictates and principles. I could even quantify my different with "suitably," "tolerably," "passably," or "reasonably." In order to find my new "different," I have to unearth fresh habits and routines to lay down the foundation for a new incarnation of myself. I have to be free to accept change and use it to move forward, proactively, to discover a unique world that is balanced, stable, secure, and compassionate.

We sense that "normal" isn't coming back,
that we are being born into a new normal:
a new kind of society, a new relationship to the earth,
a new experience of being human.
—CHARLES EISENSTEIN

ALL YOU NEVER WANTED
TO KNOW ABOUT GRIEF

I RECENTLY PASSED THE two-year marker date of Peter's death, and I looked back at my blogs, which reflect my roller coaster of a journey through grief. My writing chronicles the ups and downs (unfortunately more downs than ups) and the slow healing process toward my new life of plausible acceptability. Grief is a long and arduous process. Grief is also a teacher who has imparted some pearls of wisdom to me as I walked its challenging path. Here are some of the things I have learned from my teacher grief:

➡ Every death is sudden.

➡ Grief is not a four-letter word. Grief is a normal response to loss.

➡ Death doesn't just happen to other people. Grief is an equal-opportunity offender.

➡ You will *never* be the same person after your loss.

➡ Grief teaches you that time doesn't heal all wounds. It is what you do with time that heals.

➡ Do not be afraid to ask for all the support you can muster in grief. You will need it. Sharing your hurt lessens the pain.

➡ Grief is not a problem to be solved. Grief is a feeling that must be felt.

➡ Grief is not a twelve-step recovery program. You don't recover from grief; you adapt.

➡ You cannot postpone grief. If you do, it will bite you where the sun don't shine.

➡ Crying immense and copious tears is important in grief. Not great on the mascara, but good for the soul.

➡ There is no expiration date or shelf life on grief. Grief outlasts a Twinkie!

➡ It is more than OK to laugh while you are grieving.

➡ In grief you lose your status, your identity, and your trust. But with self-compassion, you can rebuild trust and identity. Status takes a bit more perseverance and a lot of understanding friends.

➡ "Normal" and "grief" should not be used together in the same sentence.

➡ Grief will change your inner circle of friends. You are not the same person. Your grief and healing process will bring you closer to some people and distance you from others.

➡ You will grieve your past, present, and future with your loved one.

➡ Life's milestones will always be tinged with bitter and then, hopefully, bittersweet emotions.

➡ Grief gives you the power to say no and take care of your needs and desires.

➡ Exercise is key to getting through the pain of grief.

➡ Grief teaches you that you are stronger than you ever envisioned.

➡ Ask for all the hugs you need. Hugs are mandatory!

➡ Grief is the new taboo. People feel weird talking about grief. If you open up, they will open up.

➡ Grief doesn't come in five neat stages. Grief is unbelievably tough and messy!

➡ The pain of grief is universal, but your journey is unique. Grief teaches you not to judge others in their grief and informs you how to be more empathic.

➡ Grief shows you that you can use your pain to do some good. Being compassionate with others makes you feel better.

➡ Grief confirms that life sucks sometimes.

➡ Grief informs you that no matter how much time you had together, you always want more.

➡ Grief instructs you that you are not in control in your journey of grief. Grieving helps you to find control again.

➡ The marker date of the death of your loved one is not an anniversary. It is another hurdle to go through and check off the list on your journey through grief.

➡ Your attitude is key in grief. It takes a while to get to the point where you can invest in the process fully, which is a requirement for your restoration.

➡ Grief teaches you to be authentic.

➡ Grief teaches you to bend flexibly into the pain so you don't break.

➡ Grief shows the way toward self-compassion.

➡ You will never stop grieving your loss. By allowing the grief process to continue, you honor your loved one, which is healing by default.

➡ Knowing that there is life after grief will keep you going.

➡ It does get better.

INVOLUNTARY MEMORIES
Grief Triggers

It's déjà vu all over again.
—YOGI BERRA

INVOLUNTARY MEMORIES OCCUR DURING the grieving process when you are faced with grief triggers that unconsciously bring up recollections of the past. They are called IAMs for involuntary aware memories or involuntary autobiographical memories. Marcel Proust was the first person to use the term "involuntary memory" in his novel *À la Recherche du Temps Perdu*, calling it the "essence of the past." I refer to them as grief triggers because they crop up spontaneously, when you least expect them. You are literally sidelined with the overwhelming feelings of involuntary memories in the shower, while driving, when listening to a sentimental song, when smelling the aroma of fresh doughnuts, or when watching a steamy love scene in a movie. Once the involuntary memories hit, they form a chain reaction, taking your breath away as you relive a recollection that brings deep and profound sadness to your very core. This chain reaction, which I dub an "aftershock," is primed by this involuntary memory, and your emotions go haywire trying to restore your equilibrium.

When I was deep in the throes of the early part of my grieving, it was all I could do to survive these aftershocks. I would be driving along, and a wave of involuntary memories would hit so hard it was as if I had been punched in the gut. I had to pull my car over to the side of the road and sob until the pain abated. These aftershocks came fast and furiously at the slightest provocation. They were unpredictable, but I realized that the hot shower brought them on most often. That was all right with me, since I was dripping with hot water and also with tears in a place that was hidden and safe.

As I began to work through my grief, I found that the aftershocks abated and the involuntary memories brought a more positive feeling. In my first and second years of grief, the memories were so painful, they knocked my socks off. Every time I thought of Peter, my eyes would brim with tears, and I would become a faucet unattractively dripping from my nose and eyes! But in my third year, I am now able to feel those involuntary memories as a connection to Peter. I find that when the grandkids and I are eating dinner together and we mention "Duke," his pet name, we laugh at how much he would have loved being at the fabulous Chinese restaurant, noisily slurping up soup dumplings. When I am getting ready to go out, I feel Peter's presence and hear him saying, "Damn, you look good!" which brings a smile to my face. When I walk along the ocean, I grin, with a few tears in my eyes, thinking of how much he would have loved to be here.

I will never lose my connection with Peter. Unexpected memories no longer devastate me, and they can actually cause me to emit a smile. I can't bring Peter back, but these momentary grief triggers can keep his memory close to my heart. As I adjust to my new life of "acceptably different," I will use these involuntary memories to help fill the void in my life without Peter. My hope is that, one day, I will be grateful for these involuntary memories that will keep Peter forever nestled in my heart.

THE OVERVIEW EFFECT
Putting Life into Perspective

Humanity must rise above the earth,
to the top of the atmosphere and beyond. For only then
will we understand the world in which we live.
—SOCRATES

"OVERVIEW EFFECT" IS A term first coined by space philosopher and author Frank White, referring to the mental clarity the astronauts felt in space when they looked at the earth as a tiny dot from above. The overwhelming and awesome feeling of the overview effect is the reality of Earth's small part in space, seen only as a tiny and delicate entity in a much bigger picture. It is the perspective to see life's fragility and fleetingness.

When Peter died, I had no perspective on life. I aimlessly flailed in a lonely world, buoyed by friends and family, trying to find my way on the path of grief. It took hard work and a crap load of courage to continue to move forward and find the correct course that would help me adapt to my new existence alone. I was blind to the big picture of life. I was numb, and I could only warily move one foot in front of the other.

Two years later, I am now able to see the overview effect on my life. I am able to take a few steps back to sniff the hell out of the roses and appreciate what my life has to offer. I am able to witness an eclipse of the sun—both physically, through protective glasses, and metaphysically, to find the wonder in life again. I am able to relish the small moments of joy life throws at me, and cherish them. In over two years of traveling through grief, I have found the perspective to view my progress on this demanding journey through the muck and mire. I am able to applaud and find the self-compassion to honor my passage. I am able to say, "Brava, Laurie. Look what you have accomplished!"

You don't need to travel in space to change your perspective on life. When you witness the amazing vision of a breathtaking sunset or wonder at the awe-inspiring panoramic view of the ocean, you know you must adapt and find a way to integrate these pleasurable moments into your life. Grief diminishes your concerns about self and renders you more altruistic by its very devastation. You witness how very diminutive your petty life was before your loss, and ergo you vow to try to enjoy what life offers, and donate to the cosmos with more good karma. You discover a new sense of how to problem-solve and adapt to your life. You discover the sacred in the mundane of daily life. You don't need to venture into space to change your perspective on life. The astronaut Edward Gibson said it best after his space odyssey: "You see how diminutive your life and concerns are compared to other things in the universe… The result is that you enjoy the life that is before you…It allows you to have inner peace."

I don't know if I have inner peace yet, but I do know that I have the strength and ability to forge forward into my new, acceptably different life. Maybe that will bring me inner peace? Who knows what life will hold for me as I move forward? I do know that I am not afraid of progressing onward, and I am maybe a little bit excited to see what befalls me as I continue on my journey of restoration.

~~~~~~

IMPERMANENCE IN GRIEF
Cherish the Here and Now

Nothing endures but change.
—HERACLITUS

EVERYTHING IS PREDISPOSED TO change. Every aspect of our lives goes through transformation. Nothing is everlasting. All physical and emotional concepts and relationships grow, change, fade, and eventually die.

To every thing there is a season,
and a time to every purpose under the heaven:
A time to be born, and a time to die;
a time to plant, and a time to pluck up
that which is planted;
A time to kill, and a time to heal;
a time to mourn, and a time to dance;
A time to cast away stones, and a time to
gather stones together; a time to embrace,
and a time to refrain from embracing;
A time to get, and a time to lose;
a time to keep, and a time to speak;
A time to love, and a time to hate;
a time of war, and a time of peace.
—ECCLESIASTES

Despite knowing about the transience of life, we still try to base our happiness on making the impermanent become permanent. We experience profound sadness while trying to control things and hoping they won't change. We can't control the fact that all things will eventually fade from existence. We can change our liaison with impermanence. We can alter our connection to the world, including our possessions, family, and friends.

By instilling mindfulness and care in our attitudes, we can alter how we value things. We have to remain in the here and now, and cherish each and every moment, knowing the acute fragility of life. If you are conscious of the fleetingness of life, you take nothing for granted. If you know that life is short, you cherish life to the max, and the world has a different outlook. Colors become more vivid, scents and aromas are enhanced, experiences are cherished in a secure bank of memories, and you can totally accept gratitude into your heart. If you think of impermanence as a sand castle, it becomes intensely clear that you must cherish its beauty in the here and now, knowing that in the next wave, it will be swept back into the sea.

Peter and I were big believers in carpe diem. We seized each day and cherished each moment, understanding the ephemerality of life. We were keenly aware of our true delight when we spent time with the grandkids; we reveled in the joy that was instilled in our hearts by doing our philanthropic work; we relished each and every delicious dish we ate; we treasured even just sitting together and watching television, although Peter had to endure more episodes of *Masterpiece Theatre* than he preferred.

When Peter died, I lost my power to be grateful. The catastrophic loss shook my power of positivity and tossed me into acute grief. Grief settled uncomfortably into my heart, and I became stuck in a way I had never experienced. But the thought that grief was impermanent helped me to change my attitude. It gave me the will to fight my way back methodically, minute by minute, hour by hour, day by day, and month by month, until I could ultimately conceptualize that my life had not been destroyed by my loss. Ever so slowly I came to realize that life was fleeting, and I had to cherish the memories of our life together and be grateful for the happiness we had shared. Little by little, I came to find pleasure again in my life, being mindful of the good things that I could savor. I had to accept that I had been radically changed as a human being. I even found a hint of promise and excitement in the possibilities that life might hold for me.

And speaking of savoring, I would like to share a memory of one of Peter's favorite foods at Thanksgiving, sweet potato soufflé. Soufflés definitely qualify as impermanent, as they deflate in a second. This particular sweet potato soufflé recipe does not have the attributes of a typical soufflé but does have the satisfying fluffiness. Peter adored this comfort-food dish and wasn't even aware that I lightened all the ingredients!

LIGHT SWEET POTATO SOUFFLÉ
SERVES: 10–12

You can reduce both the fat and the calories in any holiday or festive dinner with this lightened version of a traditional sweet potato pudding. Cream has been set aside in favor of 1 percent milk, and both the butter and the amounts of sugar have been greatly reduced. The result is amazingly smooth and delicious, and it qualifies as serious comfort food. Do not use a food processor or blender, which will cause the potatoes to be gluey or pasty.

- 5½ pounds large sweet potatoes or yams
- 2 tablespoons unsalted butter
- ¾ cup 1 percent milk, warmed
- 3 eggs, at room temperature
- ½ cup dark brown sugar, firmly packed
- 2 teaspoons grated orange rind
- ½ teaspoon ground cinnamon
- ½ teaspoon grated nutmeg
- salt to taste
- *Optional Topping:* 2 cups mini marshmallows

1. Bake, boil, or microwave the potatoes until soft. Peel and place them in the bowl of an electric mixer.

2. Preheat the oven to 350°F. Coat a large 2-quart casserole or rectangular or oval baking dish with nonstick cooking spray.

3. In an electric mixer, beat the cooked potatoes with the butter. Add the warmed milk, eggs, brown sugar, orange rind, cinnamon, nutmeg, and salt, and continue to beat until smooth.

4. Pour the mixture into the prepared casserole and bake for 40 minutes.

5. For an added treat, top the casserole with mini marshmallows and return it to the oven for 3 to 4 minutes, or until just golden, watching carefully to avoid burning.

6. Serve hot.

Do-Ahead Prep: The recipe can be prepared a day in advance, poured in the prepared casserole, covered, and refrigerated for one day before baking.

THE TIMELESSNESS OF GRIEF

True love cannot grow old; it is timeless.
—MATSHONA DHLIWAYO

SO MUCH OF OUR lives revolves around instant gratification. Instead of pacing our lives and enjoying the moments, we live abbreviated lives, cut short for expediency, leaving us with half-assed feelings that are never complete. We live a CliffsNotes existence without the depth of a full life. We compete for what we want instantly, and once we have it, we look toward the next acquisition like a conqueror acquiring land.

When I grew up, we conveyed our feelings through slow-paced snail mail. I loved my stationery with my name emblazoned on the top. I enjoyed writing thank-you notes, even though my handwriting resembled an illegible scrawl. I loved to write a note of appreciation to a friend who had done something cool. As a little girl, I even relished writing letters from camp detailing all the things I hated about my bunk, the counselors, the hike day, the bugs, and the weather. Kvetchy letters are still expressions of emotions that allow the writer and the reader to experience it all at a slow and leisurely tempo.

With the invention of e-mail, we have forevermore altered the rhythm and cadence of our lives. And with the addition of texting, we have made conveying messages even speedier. Everything in our lives is instant and quick. We have instant oatmeal, instant ramen, and instant frozen meals, but thankfully instant coffee is a thing of the past, gone and forgotten!

This quickened pace can spill over into the journey down the ponderous road of grief. Believe me, I searched for a way to speed my journey, rushing around, frantically looking for some quick-relief type of painkiller formula to make it all go away. But there is no quick fix in grief. Many experiencing deep losses say they don't have the time to put into grief. They want to get over it and find a quick fix to move on. I have learned that if you put a small Band-Aid on the big pain of grief, you simply create more grief for yourself.

We live in a world that is measured by velocity. The slow pace of grief does not conform to the *Fast and the Furious* generation. The pace of grief is akin to that of a tortoise, slowly putting one foot in front of the other, traversing through the dense jungle of heartache, passing by the branches of pain, looking to find a light at the end of the journey. You have to learn to respect the process because when you find nobility in it, you can truly honor your loved one. Peter would be so proud that I am pacing myself and not putting a statute of limitations on my grief.

The thing that keeps me moving forward is the knowledge that Peter would be the first person to tell me to charge ahead. He would tell me to get off my ass and be happy. This is my sacred rite of passage into my new, different life, and I will worship at the altar of grief for as long as I need, but not a minute longer.

THE PHOENIX RISING
FROM THE ASHES OF GRIEF
How to Create Meaning from Loss

As the legend goes,
when the Phoenix resurrects from the flames,
she is even more beautiful than before.
—DANIELLE LAPORTE

AS EARLY AS 500 BC, legends decreed that the ancient mythical creature, the phoenix, a legendary bird, would live for five hundred years. Near the end of its life, the phoenix would build a funeral pyre for itself, and as it began to die, it would lie down on the wood and burst into flames, to be consumed by the fire. Immediately the phoenix would reemerge renewed from the purifying ashes, more beautiful and regal than before, and live for another five hundred years, and the process would repeat perpetually. The symbolism of the phoenix is legendary. The Greeks named it the phoenix, but it is associated with the Egyptian Benu bird, the Jewish Milcham, the Persian Simurgh, the Native American Thunderbird, the Russian Firebird, the Chinese Feng Huang, and the Japanese HoHo bird. No matter what the culture, the phoenix or a similar avian-type figure remains a symbol of resurrection after loss.

For me, the phoenix has become a symbol of transformation in grief. After Peter died, I was engulfed in the flames of sorrow. I was consumed by the power of the inferno of pain, and I burned with grief. Actually,

I was burned out by grief! I could not fathom the thought of rising from the ashes of devastation. The darkness descended and erased all joy from my life. Everyday chores became insurmountable. I had lost joy, happiness, and beauty. I knew I had to find the courage to channel my inner phoenix and rise triumphantly—or at least rise to the best of my abilities—from the ashes of grief.

My transformation was not instantaneous by any means. Bit by bit, piece by piece, building block by building block, I began to emerge from the fires of devastation. I devoured books on grief, looking for answers. In those books I discovered others in similar circumstances, which brought me a modicum of relief. I asked for help, I got support, and I began to perform spiritual alchemy, to transmute my negatives into positives. I learned that by writing and helping others, I could emerge from the ashes by doing something meaningful with my life. I didn't just want to survive grief, which has pejorative vibes. Surviving was not enough for Laurie. I wanted to transform my pain and find a purpose for living again. I wanted to find pleasure, wonder, and beauty, and more importantly, I wanted to be able to say I experienced joy again. I wanted to honor Peter in the only way I knew how, by living a life worthy of him. Creating meaning from loss is my resurrection from the debris of my heartache.

A SIGH IS NOT A SIGH
Using a Sigh or Two

You must remember this
A kiss is just a kiss, a sigh is just a sigh.
The fundamental things apply
As time goes by.
—HERMAN HUPFELD, FROM THE MOVIE *CASABLANCA*

I WAS ALWAYS A sigher. I sighed in frustration when I had a glitch with my computer. I sighed happily when I saw love scenes in the movies. I sighed in annoyance when I was overwhelmed by the bills I had to pay. I sighed with a sense of relief when I finished a workout. Man, did I sigh! But most importantly, I sighed blithely every time Peter walked through the door. It wasn't a sigh of frustration; this was a sigh of pleasure and contentedness. I knew my love, my protector, my sweet husband, was home. The feeling of security was enough to make me exhale a gratifying sigh. That was the "boy, life is good" sigh." And there used to be the sigh for "thank goodness that horrible thing didn't happen to me." But Peter died, and no amount of saying kenahora (Yiddish for "evil eye"), or knocking on wood, could change this life-altering occurrence.

"To sigh" is defined as "to let out one's breath audibly, as from sorrow, weariness, or relief." Sighing involves inhaling, exhaling, or a combo of both and is unique in every person. When one sighs, it usually has some heavy emotion beneath it. Physically we don't need to sigh, since it is not part of breathing. Sighing is more of a psychological expression. It demonstrates emotionally how we are feeling at a particular moment, as if we are saying, "Phew, glad I finished that blog!"

The Norwegian scientist Karl Teigen did a series of studies with students at the University of Oslo to explore the context in which people sigh. He wanted to find out when people sigh and how the sighs are perceived by others. According to the study, a sigh is an expression of resignation and frustration, but it all depends on who is sighing, what the context is that makes the person sigh, and how the sighing is perceived by others. Another study, by Elke Vlemincx and her colleagues at the University of Leuven in Belgium, suggests that sighing acts as a physical and mental Reset button. Vlemincx felt that when you breathe in one state for too long, the lungs become stiffer and less efficient in gas exchange. Adding a sigh to the normal pattern stretches the lungs' air sacs and thus gives a sense of relief.

A sigh can be akin to the word "maybe." There is a flexibility that becomes available with the power of the word. It allows one to take a breath, or a sigh, before answering. If I can sigh and say "maybe," I am leaving myself open to other solutions or answers. "Maybe" gives us the power to be more accommodating in our approach to a problem. "Maybe" gives us a freedom from answering yes or no right away, and thereby allows us to take care of our personal needs and wants thoughtfully.

Now that I am well into the process of grief, I have found the power of the sigh, and the word "maybe," to be positive factors. I agree that a good sigh can reduce stress and help me to move forward. A sigh is a respite, which gives me time to regroup and find the resilience to fight. When I sigh, I am pressing the Pause button to breathe until I can continue. I sigh, and sigh again, and then go to my computer to write down my feelings. Yes, I sigh all the while, sometimes at my misspellings and autocorrect, but mainly at the ability to release my thoughts through sighing and to forge ahead on my journey to my new life of acceptably different.

CALL ME MAYBE

(Can I Really Be Quoting Carly Rae Jepsen?)
Using Maybe as a Pause Button

WHEN YOU ARE IN the process of grieving a loss of any kind, you must avoid looking ahead into the future. You are so devastated by the loss that you cannot envision the life that might have been. Your memories with your loved one are over, and you must find your way through the path of the present in order to venture forward. Your need for the terra firma of certitude can cloud your thinking, and your focus must be myopically limited to the now.

I proffer that the use of the word "maybe" might be of help. The word appeared between 1375 and 1425, derived from the late Middle English phrase "may be." It means possibly or perhaps. "Maybe" is the bridge between despair and hope. When you are in the midst of a journey through grief, if you look to the future, you might say, "I will be alone forever," or "How will I get through this?" But if you were to say, "Maybe things might not be so bad," you can open a world of possible options that are more hopeful. The negative attitude in your head might be transformed so that you can observe what lies ahead: "Maybe I will be OK," or "Maybe if I go through this process, I will find joy again." Instead of being mired in unnecessary angst over what could happen, if you say "maybe," you can see a glimmer of hope on the horizon. "Maybe" opens one up to the possibility of change as an adventure, rather than a fearful endeavor. "Maybe" is the link between being afraid, stuck in the endless unconstructive internal dialogue swirling in your head, and the path that is open and full of potentially happy possibilities.

I like using the word "maybe," which affords me the time to regroup and think about whether I really want to accept an invitation. When in grief, you have to be able to take care of yourself. Sometimes, a direct no is a bit harsh. "Maybe" makes it easier to hit the Pause button and think. When I am asked if I want to attend an event, I might say, "Maybe, if I can work out the timing." By using "maybe" as a breathing space, I can take the time to assess whether I really want to attend. I also use "maybe" as a tool instead of fretting over the minutiae of life. If I am worrying over a doctor's appointment or even something as mundane as bad traffic, I try to turn my worry upside down and say, "Maybe I will sail straight through on the freeway today." Using the word "maybe" can be a meditative technique to find positivity in stress.

"Maybe" can also have a negative connotation, as when we asked our parents if we could go for ice cream and they said "maybe," meaning "not a shot!" There are the musings and wonderings around the word— for instance, we might think, "If Sonny Corleone in *The Godfather* had used E-ZPass, maybe he would still be alive." When you are at the doctor's office, you might ask, "Will it hurt?" The doctor might answer, "Maybe." Ouch!

I am going to adopt "maybe" as a positive tool to help me find balance in my life. If I start to get obsessed with thoughts of sadness, I will try to breathe and remember the hope "maybe" engenders in me. The word gives me the wherewithal to step back and be kind to others. Being immersed in "maybe," I can see hope, or at least I can see a light to guide me through the rest of my journey of grief. Maybe it won't work out? But knowing that the ride will be interesting and transformative boosts my confidence and optimism.

~~~~~~

DON'T WORRY, BABY
Living in the Present in Grief

Do not anticipate trouble, or worry about
what may never happen. Keep in the sunlight.
—BENJAMIN FRANKLIN

"WORRY" IS DEFINED AS "giving way to anxiety or unease." Worry is allowing one's mind to dwell on difficulties and misfortunes. It is the state of fretting, stressing out, stewing over something, and tormenting oneself. Simply put, it is getting your panties in a bunch! When you experience the death of a loved one, the trauma of that momentous and horrible event unleashes a torrent of worries that takes you to new heights of anxiety. The worries you are facing are not inconsequential or trifling. Your apprehension and misgivings are more than valid, since your life has been uprooted and turned completely upside down.

With the death of a spouse, you suddenly have to figure out how you can go on alone. You ponder what will happen to you. You wonder, "WTF will happen when I get sick and have no one to care for me?" You want to know whether you have the finances to make it. You need to know how to deal with the sudden loneliness. You must evaluate how to start your life again as a single person.

When Peter died, I worried about all of this. I went down the road of catastrophizing on many an occasion, and broke into an unbearable sweat. I created my own storm and then got really pissed off when it rained. Worry was a catalyst to negativity, and I had to head it off at the pass and stop looking to the future. I had to put the toxic worry out of my head and figure out a way to face my new life without added stress. I had to trust in the process and believe that my life would evolve organically. I had to remember that looking ahead to this new, different life had no positive value. Basically, I had to stop agonizing about the future and pay proper tribute to the present.

I am not good at meditation. I really wish I could utter "om" and chant, but the chattering monkeys in my brain keep my mind whirling with ideas. To help with my distress, I decided to worry efficiently and set aside a limited worry time in a hand-picked worry place. The place I chose was a hot shower. I read that the heat of the warm water unleashes dopamine in the brain and creates a feeling of relaxation. I figured if I worried in the shower, maybe I could relax into the anxiety and find some sanity in my angst. I also decided I could worry while walking, particularly with a friend. Exercise was my ticket to rational thinking and lucidity. Talking the problems out with a friend was an ideal way to put my worry to bed, or at least tuck it in for the night.

Writing was also a way for me to face my worries head on. When I wrote down my fears, I could look back and face them fully until they became less terrifying. I could tackle them one by one, and as I typed away, they seemed to dissipate. Maybe putting them on paper helped me to visualize the anxiety, and therefore made the fears seem less scary. When I write about the worst-case scenario, I can devise concrete plans to discuss with my friends or a counselor, or just put a positive spin on my apprehensions. I was still petrified that something bad would happen, but writing it down somehow communicated to my brain that I was powerless to change it. This process released my worry a bit—not completely, but it made my worries abate and seem surmountable.

When I go down the path to a tributary I call "worry mania," I know that if I take deep breaths, it can slow down the avalanche of fearful thoughts and catapult me back to the present. Another trick I have used is to make a collage. I go through magazines, pick pictures that depict my thoughts, and put them together until the trepidation and apprehension have abated. I sincerely promise that I won't exhibit these odd collages, but they have helped me to put my terror into perspective, and they keep my mind from going down the road to the futile land of catastrophe.

If you must worry, why not do it over a pot of soup, which will help to ease your troubles? My favorite soup is a wonderful Tuscan dish called ribollita, which is easy to prepare and will cause you no worries!

~~~~~~

RIBOLLITA
SERVES: 8

Ribollita, which means "boiled again" in Italian, is a hearty Tuscan-style bean-and-cabbage soup that is thickened with bread. Tuscan cooks say that you should start cooking the soup one day and finish it the next. This is a great winter lunch or supper dish that is meant to be cooked to a thick and flavorful consistency.

The soup requires a lot of chopping chores but can be prepared several days in advance.

2 teaspoons extra-virgin olive oil
1 medium onion, finely chopped
2 ribs celery, finely chopped
2 medium carrots, peeled and finely chopped
2 cloves garlic, finely minced
4 cups defatted chicken broth
1 14½-ounce can diced-fire-roasted-tomatoes, including liquid
3 cups shredded Savoy cabbage
1 6-ounce package baby spinach
2 tablespoons chopped fresh Italian parsley
2 teaspoons minced fresh sage
2 teaspoons minced fresh thyme leaves
salt and freshly ground pepper to taste
1 15-ounce can cannellini or Great Northern beans, drained
4–6 1-inch-thick slices day-old Italian bread, cut into 1-inch chunks
Garnish: chopped Italian parsley, freshly grated lemon zest, and freshly grated Parmesan cheese

1. In a nonstick Dutch oven or large saucepan, heat the oil to medium and sauté the onion, celery, and carrots, stirring often, until softened, about 5 to 6 minutes. Add the garlic and stir to combine.

2. Add the broth, tomatoes, cabbage, spinach, parsley, sage, thyme, salt, and pepper. Bring to a boil, cover, reduce heat, and simmer for 2 hours, or until the vegetables are very tender.

3. Stir in the beans and bread and continue to cook for about 30 minutes, or until the bread dissolves into the soup.

4. Serve hot in deep soup bowls garnished with the parsley, lemon zest, and Parmesan cheese.

Notes: Green beans, Swiss chard, kale, potatoes, zucchini, and other seasonal vegetables can be added to the soup. When adding extra vegetables, add enough broth to keep the ribollita thick but still soupy.

YOU KNOW YOU'RE GETTING BETTER WHEN...

I HAVE PROCESSED MY grief by blogging constantly, taking baby steps toward my restoration with occasional tumbles along the way. When you are doing grief work, it is difficult to see the signs of improvement, so I decided to chronicle my improvements in a game I call "I Know I'm Getting Better When..."

I KNOW I'M GETTING BETTER WHEN...

➡ I can look at Peter's picture and not weep.

➡ I can spend time alone and be content puttering around at home.

➡ I can watch a suspenseful show like *The Americans* without reaching for Peter's comforting hand.

➡ I can go on a plane and not shake in fear as the turbulence hits, without missing Peter's hand in mine.

➡ I don't pounce on someone who says, "I know how you feel."

➡ I can live in the now. The long view sucks.

➡ I can anticipate Thanksgiving without tearing up at the thought of Peter's plate full of sweet potatoes and marshmallows.

➡ I can tame the chattering monkeys in my head through mindfulness. (Sadly, still working on the meditation issue. Om)

➡ I can sleep through the night without pharmaceuticals, booze, or weed.

➡ I can take a walk on a crisp day and feel good, all by myself.

➡ I notice that time doesn't drag as much, and the weekends aren't as long.

➡ I can reconcile the bank statements by myself. (I lie. This will never happen, and Peter would have been laughing at the concept.)

➡ I can say no to toxic friendships without guilt. Saying no can be so empowering!

➡ I can laugh out loud at a joke and actually enjoy it.

➡ I can use the widow card wisely, especially when dealing with the telephone company.

➡ I have fewer grief bursts in the car or the shower.

➡ I am actually really hungry. Cacio al pepe. Yum!

➡ I realize that the word "denial" doesn't stand for "don't even notice I am lying."

➡ I can watch the Oakland Raiders win and not miss seeing Peter's big grin.

➡ I don't miss his five daily check-in calls.

➡ I can phone a friend to fill that void.

➡ I can stop to smell the flowers and actually enjoy them.

➡ I can take a walk on the beach without tearing up.

➡ I can concentrate and focus enough to read a book.

➡ I can order a burger and fries without thinking of his smile. Yes, a turkey burger, but I can still smile.

➡ I can comfort others in the same vortex of grief.

➡ I can watch *The Way We Were* and not curl into a ball of pain.

➡ I can watch *Young Frankenstein* and laugh out loud without tearing up when Peter doesn't say, "Put the candle back!"

➡ I can truly look forward to getting up in the morning.

➡ I can find growth from my loss. (This one will take a lot more work!)

➡ I finally reach a place in my life where I feel good enough that I can cease blogging about my pain.

➡ I can tell grief, who has moved in as a tenant, to vacate the premises, or at least take a shorter lease.

➡ I can recover the "me" that went with him.

➡ I can bounce forward!

~~~~~~

DIVERSIONARY ACTIVITIES
Discovering Pleasurable Distractions

STRUGGLING THROUGH GRIEF CAN be exhausting and pretty
much the pits. It is hard work, and it takes all the energy you can summon up, especially in the early stages. You can only do so much grief
work at once. It is key to have diversionary activities to allow you the
strength and fortitude to persevere through the muck and mire.

Here are a few positive distracting pursuits that I recommend to help
you through your journey of grief:

➡ Shuffle the Beatles' songs. Listening to John,
George, Paul, and Ringo can only lift your mood.
"I Want to Hold Your Hand," "Strawberry Fields
Forever," "All My Loving," "All You Need Is Love,"
and "We Can Work It Out" put me on a high no
matter what mood has clouded my thinking. If you
want peppier, try Meghan Trainor, Queen, the
Eagles, or the Rolling Stones.

➡ Take a walk, preferably at the beach. The wind, the
sun, and nature act as an instant mood enhancer.
I sometimes cry on my beach walk, thinking of the
times Peter and I walked together, but it is a great
tool to add resilience and courage to your well-being.

➡ Journalize. Putting your feelings down on paper can
somehow move them out of your brain and onto

the paper, and perhaps it can help to allow room for a more positive attitude.

➡ Laugh! Mel Brooks, Mel Brooks, Mel Brooks! Nothing beats a day vegging while watching *Blazing Saddles*, *Young Frankenstein*, or *Spaceballs*. Telling a joke, preferably a dirty one, is always good for the psyche.

➡ Listen to podcasts. *Serial* and *S-Town* are guaranteed to make you forget for a while, and give you a break.

➡ Binge-watch TV. Bingeing on British mysteries is good for the soul and the brain. I signed up for Acorn TV, which allowed me to see all fifty-seven episodes of Australia's answer to *Downton Abbey*, called *A Place to Call Home*.

➡ Knit. I might look a bit like Madame Defarge, but knitting is calming, particularly when watching British mysteries.

➡ Cook. Prepping in the kitchen is therapy for me, but I know it's not for everyone. The chopping, the sautéing, the whole culinary gestalt is a great diversion.

➡ Read. It was hard for me to focus on reading in the early stages of grief. Instead I used audio books, which were a great distraction. Now I am able to concentrate more and love reading historical novels, particularly ones that involve the World War II era.

➡ Movies. Going out to the movies, munching on big bags of buttered popcorn, and getting engrossed in a thriller or romcom does much for healing the soul. I am lucky enough to take a movie class at UCLA Extension called Sneak Previews, which shows first-run films with speakers after.

➡ Artistic pursuits. I wish I had a scintilla of artistic talent in my being, but right now I can only recommend this to others. The only artistic pursuit I can do is coloring, but I don't quite grasp its supposed healing qualities.

➡ Travel. Getting away is the best diversion. I like to travel to New York City, where I have friends and can forget myself while going to the theater, eating at restaurants, and walking the streets for hours.

➡ Helping others. Finding a way to help others is not only diverting but satisfying, and it is great for building self-compassion.

~~~~~~

CINDERELLA LOOKING
FOR PRINCE CHARMING?

ONCE UPON A TIME *there was a pretty-good-looking princess named Laurie, who serendipitously met her handsome Prince Charming named Peter. She swooned at his kindness, sense of humor, love of all things edible (excluding veggies), and gorgeous head of hair. He fell in love with her blond tresses even with the peroxide applications, her laughter, and her long legs, amply visible in a 1960s rabbit miniskirt. They were thunderstruck by a bolt of love beyond anything that either of the Brothers Grimm could have conjured up. What really happened was that they fit together like a tight puzzle, interlocking all the pieces of their psyches. They became a close-knit team, and it lasted for a very, very, very long time, but sadly did not end in happily ever after. Now Laurie is an older princess, perhaps a duchess (with no dowager hump or facial warts), without her Prince Charming to make her feel loved. She no longer is taken into Prince Peter's big loving arms and held. She no longer feels safe and protected. Her fable has not ended happily.*

My journey of grief has taken me on a windy and circuitous route, with bumpy and jarring rides of tears and plunges into deep chasms of sadness. Some days I am fine, and I can actually feel that I just might come out of this funk and be OK. Some days I am not cool, but I function, and I move through my process in hopes of...what? Aha, that is the $64,000 question. What is it that I hope for in my future? Is it a Prince Charming? Would he look like Cary Grant or Marilyn Manson?

I know this sounds off-the-wall crazy, but grief has inserted me into the first act of *Cinderella*, and I am having a challenging time extricating myself out of act one and moving on to the good parts. I do the relentless work of grieving by cleaning the floors of my soul and washing the windows of my heart, but I am still stalled in a melancholy life. It is the loneliness that is the killer in this process I call my "after life"—life after Peter. Being alone is the hardest hurdle I have to overcome. I am able to write publicly and openly about my grief process, but when I come home to an empty house, that feeling of alienation rears its ugly head. I would love to fast-forward to the end of the fairy tale and find a Prince Charming, but this seems illusory. I know I could never replace Peter, but I would like to find someone with whom to share a laugh, enjoy a dinner out, and find an antidote to the lonesomeness that has plagued me since Peter died. Sure, I would love to find a Prince Charming, but that is a fantasy I have to take off the table.

Basically, I have two doors to try. Door number one is a path in which I constantly seek another man to satisfy my loneliness. If I go through that door, I will go online and search for a partner, and never be satisfied until I find one to fill the void, no matter the quality. It reminds me of staying in the Ramada Inn in the 1970s, when they embroidered "luxury for less" on the towels. I don't want a second-rate prince! I want a real, live, full-fledged, top-notch, quality human male with whom I can share my life! Door number two allows me the wiggle room to find that part of myself that will make me happy enough, and if Prince Charming were to walk through, it wouldn't be so terrible! For now, I choose door number two, and I will take my chances with me, myself, and I.

THE DUALITY OF
A GRIEVING HEART
The Yin and Yang of Grief

DUALITY IS THE CIRCUMSTANCE or condition of being dual. It is an instance of opposition or contrast between two concepts. It is the yin and the yang. It is two sides of a coin. For widows this polarity is both the pain of loss and the joy of remembrance. As a widow takes her journey and begins to move forward, there is a duality in merging her previous life with her spouse, and progressing towards her new solo existence. As time goes by, the feeling of duality comingles one's new life with the memories of one's old life.

When you begin a new relationship, you can hear your love saying, "Right on." When I had to break up with a guy after a few dates, it was Peter who said, "He's not good enough for you, my love. Dump the SOB." The duality of my life is blending together as I move forward with heartbreak and also joy. I am learning to exist in the world of now while clinging to the memories of my wonderful marriage. This is the duality of a grieving heart.

I liken my duality to a shrapnel wound. When Peter died, there was an explosion in my heart, and the sharp, jagged pieces of my former love got embedded deep into my heart. The pain of the explosion was so horrific, I didn't know if I could move forward. I was keenly aware that it was too dangerous to remove these jagged pieces, so I learned to live with the sting and soreness and adapt to a life with this sorrow locked inside me. Sometimes the pain throbs unexpectedly at anniversaries or when I hear Sarah McLachlan's "I Will Remember You." But I have learned to move forward, with the knowledge that I have remembrance pieces of our love tucked neatly inside my heart.

The shrapnel is a good image for me to grasp. The shrapnel is inside me, and like grief, I have to let the pain of it ease on its own timetable. I have been educated in a full course of grief. I have earned a major in melancholy and a minor in sadness. The pain is a reminder of my love and my memories of my former life, but it is also a way of keeping Peter close to me as a trusted adviser as I move ahead. I am living with the dichotomy of pain in the form of the shrapnel and the longing to move forward, but I know that I have wise counsel and memories to help me on my journey. I have to be a champion of my own life. I have to play out the repellent cards that have been dealt to me. I have to fight for my survival and live according to Nora Ephron's wise counsel: "Above all, be the heroine of your life, not the victim."

HOW TO COPE WITH A WEDDING ANNIVERSARY
AFTER THE DEATH OF YOUR SOULMATE

WHEN I MET AND married my soulmate, Peter, over fifty years ago at the age of 23, I knew I had found the person who would cherish me unconditionally in sickness and in health. We met on October 17, 1967. We were engaged two months later and married two months after that. I knew I had found the man who wouldn't stop saying to me that he had lived life fully with the woman he loved.

Before Peter's sudden and unexpected death, we had indulged in many a discussion about our impending fiftieth wedding anniversary. We were so looking forward to celebrating this momentous occasion and had been buzzing with ideas of how we wanted to commemorate the date. We thought of traveling, although Peter was not big on schlepping on planes and abhorred the hassle of the lines at airports. He used to refer to the TSA as "thousands standing around." I like travel although my packing skills are pathetic and I go by the mantra that "an item left at home is not a worthy item." This philosophy results in the unfortunate fact that my suitcase often outweighs a sumo wrestler which is definitely not a plus on my aching back! We mused over throwing a big bash for our fiftieth, but that didn't seem to be a proper way to honor just the two of us and our incredible union. The option that seemed perfect was a road trip where we could relax and celebrate with walks on the beach, dinners with lots of wine, and just enjoy each other's company to the max.

After Peter's death, our wedding anniversary was forever changed. The once anticipated event that celebrated our unique and amazing love was now a dreaded occasion. We had both looked forward to shouting to the world that we had made it to fifty years and counting. The second Peter died, February 11th had pain written all over it. The days leading up to this milestone were the toughest to face. I knew I had to confront the hurt head on, which took a toll on my sleeping, eating, and health. I got a bad cold from the stress and was weepy which didn't help the fact that I was already sneezing and dripping like a faucet. Score one for tissues with extra aloe and lotion!

I knew that I had to formulate a plan to get me through this significant milestone. I recently joined the board of a wonderful organization call *Our House Grief Support Center* which had been my go to place after Peter died, providing the grief support I needed in a group situation, as well as other resources. The date of my first board retreat was, you got it, my fiftieth anniversary. Being with people who understood my angst was actually a good way to honor the date. I lit a candle and talked about Peter and our extraordinary love. In an instant I was comforted by a blanket of new, but amazingly caring individuals.

When I got home after a full day full of tumultuous emotions, I was filled with a sense that my love for Peter didn't stop at forty-seven years. My love for him has grown in a unique way. If it is possible, I am more in love with Peter now than when he was alive. I am keenly aware that keeping the memory of our love alive is in my court. But, sometimes I feel him around me, helping me, guiding me, and pumping me up with enough resilience to move forward.

Peter was my prince, my knight in shining armor; my champion; my best friend; and my rock who I will love until I take my last breath.

A GLIMMER OF HOPE
Keeping Your Negative Feelings in Check

There is nothing good or bad, but thinking makes it so.
—WILLIAM SHAKESPEARE

AFTER THE TWO-YEAR MARK of Peter's death, I was hit with a profound sadness that I couldn't overcome. I spent the first year just getting through the pain. During the second year, I struggled to absorb reality and its heartbreaking ramifications. But in the third year, I was knocked for a loop by a system-wide feeling of melancholy. I decided to try to discover why I was so filled with sorrow. I know the obvious, that reality is even clearer after time passes, but somehow, I was letting negative emotions take over my sense of reason. I was tossing myself a pity party and indulging in the negative feelings that I would always be alone. These discouraging emotions were like needy little minions. They multiplied and insinuated themselves into my thought processes. They grumbled and mistreated the happier positive feelings, leaving no room for hope or even a scintilla of optimism. The minions of anxiety wanted to be heard, and they created an unhealthy atmosphere in my head. They took up residence in my brain, leaving little room for anything but worry, sadness, and a pungent aroma of gloom. I was stuck in the Mel Brooks movie *High Anxiety* and unable to set myself free.

One day I realized that I had to keep these negative feelings in check. These unhopeful emotions were clearly clouding my vision and preventing positive sensations from developing. I had to push the minions of pessimism into a corral where I could cordon off their unsightly behavior to allow progressive and upbeat thinking to be nurtured. I basically had to rewire my brain and avoid the pitfalls of the path to gloom and doom. Once I had corralled the minions and put them in check, I decided to imagine a different scenario. The new scenario allowed me to have a glimmer of hope. I had to summon my favorite word, "maybe," and put a positive spin on my thoughts. I had to ask myself, "What are the odds that you might find another relationship?" I had to admit to 50/50 or at least 40/60. Those odds struck a note of hopefulness in my head. Was it possible that maybe I might find love again?

Then I added Peter to the mix. What would Peter say about this revolting development I was mired in? I decided to conjure up Peter and his wisdom, and I began to fantasize about Peter being the arbiter and coordinator of my new hope. Peter was a list maker and organizer who would have strategized a plan of attack. Here is Peter's imaginary letter as the best cheerleader ever, even in absentia:

> *Dear Laurie,*
>
> *You can do this! You must create a happy life for yourself. In your heart, you know that I am cheering you on to find joy. You go, girl!*
>
> *Write about your feelings and see if you can better understand them. Remember to write on the computer because your handwriting sucks!*
>
> *Practice self-compassion and try to keep the minions of negative emotions at bay. Remember, I always thought you were hot! Keep that thought, my love.*
>
> *Ask your friends if they might know someone fabulous for you to date. At our age, that is basically anyone with a pulse. Just kidding!*
>
> *I know you hate the Internet, but you need to put yourself out there. Sift through the Dumpster diving and see if you can find someone special. Remember, no actors!*

*Pat yourself on the back for at least trying to find some-
one on Match.com! But after listening to the podcast
about the Internet predator Dirty John, I realized maybe
dating websites might not be such a great idea. My bad.*

*Every time you feel sad, remember the odds. You said
there was a 50/50 chance, so believe it.*

*Be grateful for something, even if it is just a great
hamburger.*

*When you feel a sense of sadness creeping into your
thoughts, remember that glimmer of hope and dangle it
as a carrot to help steady your head.*

*The world is full of karma. Do something kind to
someone else, and you will receive good karma in return.*

Know that I will always be in your heart forever.

Love, Your Petey

TO DATE, OR NOT TO DATE?
THAT IS THE QUESTION

I HAVE COME TO the point in my journey where friends and family are encouraging me to date. Even I, can finally get my head around the fact that I am ready to start meeting a potential partner. But the thought of jumping into the dating pool is enough to make me curl into a ball and suck my thumb. Fifty years ago, people met in bars or were fixed up by friends. Today, you have to go online, make a profile without lying too much about your age, put up some pictures that make you look hot (or at least acceptable), and then wait to be "winked" at or "faved," or worse, swiped off the face of the app!

Many widows and widowers feel that dating is a betrayal of their loved ones. Some feel that it is exhausting to start over and make small talk when conversation flowed so easily in a marriage. Many don't feel they can ever replace their loved one. Grief is unique to everyone. There is no magic answer to the question "How do you know when it is time to date?" Finding the right time to start dating after a loss should be up to you, and you alone. Shoulds must be tossed out the window. Try not to listen to others who say it is time you started dating. They are not in your shoes. This is a complex and difficult step in your journey of grief. You must be the arbiter of this decision. You must weigh the pros and cons and examine all the reasons you are finally ready, or decide whether it might be too soon to venture into the dating world, where you are out there and subject to rejection and possibly further pain. You have to be strong enough in your own self-worth before you can fly away from the nest of grief into the newfangled dating arena of today. You clearly must fortify yourself against the negative pitfalls of being rebuffed.

It is over two years since Peter died, and I am at last venturing into the dating world. I am ready to do this because I know that Peter would be the first one to tell me to be happy. After two years of grieving, I know he would want me to venture out and try to meet someone who would make me laugh again or at least buy me a nice dinner! I am aware that dating is not the cure for loneliness, but I might find someone to add joy to my life. I was definitely ready to try. I made sure to be up front with my family, and they were on board with me getting out there.

Since the dating pool at my age is pathetic, I decided to join a dating site to widen my horizons. If I am to find companionship, then I have to venture out and experience online dating. Besides, the laughs alone had to be worth it. My girlfriend and I checked out the possible candidates on JDate, and we fell off our chairs in guffaws, so I decided to try a site geared to the over fifty set. Setting up my profile was quite the task. I had to fill in lots of questions. The first question was "Looking For," and the choices were marriage, serious relationship, travel partner, casual (I assume this is dating-site code for "hookup"), friends (with or without benefits), or pen pal. Why would I plunk down money for a dating website for a pen pal? I had one of those in grade school, and she lived in Denmark! I filled all the requisite boxes, put up a few pics, and paid for a few months. Within seconds a barrage of pictures of elderly gentlemen way over fifty appeared on my "views list." I realized they were retirees, but didn't they have anything better to do than troll this website at 7:30 a.m.? I was hit on by eighty-five-year-olds and forty-five-year-olds. Who knew I was a cougar? Lucky me! I eliminated all the right wingers; the ones who hadn't finished high school; those who were never married; the "social smokers"; those who loved their cats, snakes, and ferrets; the one who put up his profile picture wearing short shorts while seated in La-Z-Boy lounger; and the one who listed his occupation as a "stay at home clown." You can't make this crap up!

After this horrific experience, I heard about a matchmaking service called "It's Just Lunch." I wanted a way to meet someone without sifting through the rubble of the Dumpster-diving dating pool. I didn't want a hookup site like Tinder that would require me to swipe prospective dates—or worse, get swiped! The interview was quite lengthy, which was a good sign. They asked me what qualities I needed in a future date, and without hesitation I said, "Politically liberal, a sense of humor, and someone that was pleasant looking and preferably taller than I." I waited for my dating consultant to call.

My first date was a disaster. It lasted under an hour. Al (names changed to protect the innocent—although not innocent in this case) greeted me by saying, "You are attractive. Why would you use a dating site?" Really? That's your opening line?

He volunteered nothing, so I asked him about his interests according to the description sent by my dating consultant.

"I hear you like cooking?"

He replied, "No way."

"I hear you are seventy," I said.

He answered, "I lied."

I said, "I hear you are recently divorced?"

He said, "I've been single for over thirty years," code for "I am looking for a hookup."

Al never looked me in the eye, never asked me anything about myself, and didn't know I was a widow, which I blame on the dating site. When the separate checks came, he didn't even look at the tab; he just said, "Separate checks, a great idea!" I understand the concept of separate checks on a first meeting, but c'mon! At least offer. This guy's largesse level in moolah and spirit was at ground zero. When I almost ran out of the restaurant after he said he didn't want coffee, he exclaimed, "Tell them you liked me so I can see you again."

Without hesitation, I scowled at him and said, "You must be joking! Not unless hell freezes over!" That is the whitewashed version of what I actually uttered! If he were an Uber or Lyft driver, I would rate him with no stars.

Date two was slightly better, but that is because the bar was so low. As I was driving to park for my date, which was dinner this time, I saw an older gentleman listing like the Leaning Tower of Pisa as he walked, trying to get to the restaurant. Yup, this was Alex, my next candidate. The old dude was four years younger than I, was sweet, and insisted that he would pick up the check. Turns out Alex had only been married once, for about a year. The evening tanked from there. There was no spark, chemistry, or even a pulse. Alex liked handicapping horses, reading, and watching television in bed while chewing Nicorette gum. I decided quickly that lunch was an easier out! Unless it is It's Just Drinks, I am not on board with It's Just Dinner!

Date three was an Australian dude who loved to pilot his canal boat in Europe. He proceeded to tell me about his multimillion-dollar ranch in Northern California, the nineteen buildings he owned in Los Angeles, and his house in Venice, California. I couldn't find a single thing we had in common except for food, which he relished as noted in his ordering of two glasses of wine, grilled salmon, and two desserts. I ordered a salad. The check came, and yup, you guessed it, he announced we were splitting it. With all his talk of money and property, he didn't even have the kindness to offer to pick up the check!

My final date followed the disaster pattern of *It's Just Lunch*. Sean arrived wearing a stained and tattered jacket over a never washed Hawaiian shirt. He was a psychologist so I thought he might be more empathetic. He never complemented me on my looks, he never made eye contact, and he never once asked me about myself. I was out of there in one interminable hour. So far, *It's Just Lunch* is out to lunch! I decided that dating sites suck at my age and that if I meet someone, it will be through a friend. Dating sites are great for younger people. At my age, they are looking for a nurse or a purse!

DATING TIPS FOR WIDOWS

➡ Everybody's grief is unique. Date when you sense you are ready, not when others proclaim you should.

➡ Only add someone to your life when you feel strong enough to stand on your own.

➡ Make sure your children and close family members are ready for this. Be up front about your plans to date.

➡ Take it slow, at a glacial pace! Baby steps are recommended.

➡ Know that it may feel weird at first, but try to go with the flow and be open to meeting someone.

➡ Online dating might resemble the dregs at the bottom of the barrell, but it is the wave of the future.

THE FIRST BOYFRIEND
The Dude

I WAS RECENTLY FIXED up with a dude. At my age, I say "dude" just because I want to sound hip to my grandkids. Since I discovered online dating to be singularly disgusting, a fix-up sounded like a good idea. The dude had texted me a few times once we set the date. Turns out the dude was funny. I love funny. Funny is good. Funny is great! The banter made me feel a bit like a teenager, which was an added benefit. I would run to my computer to see if he had e-mailed with more banter. At my age, banter is the closest to sexting I will ever get!

I met the dude at a restaurant, and he was pleasant looking. We talked easily, and the banter continued. We both loved food, wine, and art. We had so many common interests. And the banter was the best part of the night. We hugged after dinner, and I smiled all the way home. I thought to myself, "I could do this again." After a few dates, the banter began in earnest. I loved the banter and his wit, but something in the back of my mind set up a red flag. Not once had he told me I was attractive. Not once had he complimented me. I was used to a man who worshipped me from the moment my head lifted from the pillow (with bed head) to the moment it touched down again at night. Each time I looked in Peter's eyes, I saw worship, adoration, and respect.

And then there was the smell. Call it chemistry, call it scent, I loved the way Peter smelled. I would soak up the scent of him, all soapy and fresh. This guy didn't smell right at all. In fact, I was actually turned off by his scent. I guess that is chemistry, and the fact that I have a very strong sense of smell came into play big time. Our pheromones (airborne chemical messengers released from the body) were definitely not in sync.

The dates continued, and things progressed, but more red flags were going up. I didn't feel cherished or adored. I felt like I had to sharpen my wit and be on guard with my answers. I didn't feel safe. When we finally kissed, there was a gruffness that scared me. Peter was a gentle kisser and lover, and that was what I had anticipated. By now the warning lights were flashing big time, and I knew it was time to call it quits.

I called him and told him, "It's not you; it's me." I know, that line has been used on many an occasion, but I really didn't want him to think it was his fault. He was taken aback and said he really wanted to see me again. I firmly ended it, and he got resentful and said, "You know, it has been two years since you were widowed. You should toughen up." Toughen up? Now I knew that the dude was wrong for me. Finished business. Over and out. Going through grief is hard enough, but telling someone to toughen up is not the sign of a caring or loving person. He was clearly threatened by the love I had with Peter. I knew I had made the right choice in stopping the relationship.

My grief therapist told me dating for a widow is like making a batch of pancakes. The first one is always lousy and has to be tossed out. She asked me what was keeping me from breaking up. I told her it was the fear that I wouldn't find someone else. Then I realized that I couldn't live in fear. I had to regain my hope for the future and the dream that I would find someone who would be kind, gentle, and caring, who would worship the ground I walked on. It's a tall order, but it's one that I hope will be fulfilled one day.

IS THERE BENEFIT IN LOSS?

Grief doesn't change you. It reveals you.
—JOHN GREEN

NOW THAT I HAVE been on my journey through grief for a considerable time, I am beginning to observe gratitude lift its lovely and gentle head. I smile at what I have accomplished and appreciate that I am forging forward. I see hints of my new personality emerging. Don't get me wrong; I would give anything, and I mean anything, to just see Peter walk through the door and smile. But I have noticed that I am finding a sense of purpose in my life that is deeper than before Peter died. I am so proud (notice I didn't say Peter would be proud) of my writing. I love the fact that I can help myself by blogging about grief, and I appreciate the added benefit of an online community who can benefit from my writing. I am rethinking and questioning my priorities and finding some slight benefits in my loss. I have opted to survive this ordeal and transcend the pain of grief. My life has a new sense of determination, and I am finding that I am evolving out of my cocoon of sadness like a butterfly making a metamorphosis to find more substance and consequence in my life.

LOSING SOMEONE YOU LOVE TEACHES YOU TO

➡ Stop and smell the roses and find joy in life. You have acquired a new conviction that you don't want to sweat the small stuff.

➡ Take nothing for granted. Be grateful for the small things in life that make you happy.

➡ Show up in your life and live fully in the present. Your past is gone, and your future is too scary to envision. You are keenly aware that you must live every moment to the fullest and stay in the present.

➡ Order your priorities. You have a new barometer for deciding what matters most and what is unimportant.

➡ Be more tender and compassionate with others.

➡ Be more self-compassionate and give yourself room to both screw up and be forgiven.

➡ Develop a heightened sense of empathy.

➡ Acquire more sensitivity in your life.

➡ Foster a sense of adventure. The fact that life is so fleeting can help you to take more risks and travel, make new friends, and be more honest with others.

➡ Use your power of choice and say no. You no longer have to pussyfoot around when making your needs known. Use "maybe" to deflect a bit, but always protect your needs and wants, and say no if it isn't right.

➡ Volunteer! There is scientific evidence that volunteering to help others helps in the grief process.

➡ Laugh more. Laughter is not only the best medicine; it is diverting and good for the whole body.

➡ Cherish your family and friends as if they were gifts.

➡ Appreciate love more. Gratefully look back at the love you shared. Life can't be controlled; it can only be embraced. Love what you have in the here and now.

➡ Take the time to tell your loved ones, "I love you."

➡ Simplify your existence. Try to rid yourself of anger, resentment, stress, and anxiety, and replace them with love, forgiveness, resilience, and gratitude.

➡ Cherish your memories as reminders of the love you shared.

➡ Realize your inner strength, look back at how far you have come, and celebrate your small victories.

➡ Develop the ability to put yourself first and see your new priorities in life.

➡ Begin to love without sorrow and remember without pain.

➡ Pat yourself on the back for being a survivor, not a victim. You will never get over your loss, but it will become part of who you are.

➡ Honor your loved one by living a full and satisfying life, with that person nestled cozily in your heart every step of the way.

Printed in Great Britain
by Amazon